The bizar

Ella Sully

by
G.M Warner

Published by G.M. Warner

Printed by Catford Print Centre, London SE6 2PN

© G.M. Warner

gill.m.warner@googlemail.com

First published in Great Britain 2015

The moral right of the author has been asserted

ISBN: 978-0-9934226-0-7

A catalogue record of this book is available from the British Library

Design by Zoë Draper

z.draper@btinternet.com

For my mother and father
with love

Contents:

Introduction

It was a blustery April day in 2012 when we parked the car in Fitzhead, a small Somerset village ten miles from Taunton and then walked the half mile or so along the lane up to Burrow Hill Farm where my great-aunt Ella had been born in one of the farm's tied cottages over a hundred years before.

It is still a quiet rural setting and looking over the ploughed fields of heavy red clay soil, I imagined Ella's father, my great-grandfather, working on the land here in this remote corner of Somerset all those years ago. He would have been digging ditches, mending fences, maybe leading a team of heavy horses in some back-breaking toil of a pre-tractor era.

I had little idea of what to expect at Burrow Hill, the farm buildings were still marked on the Ordnance Survey map but it might be a private house or holiday home. As we approached Burrow Hill it became clear that this was still a working farm; the old farmhouse itself was well-maintained and several men were working with fork-lift trucks in the outlying barns and yard. And then the strangest thing ~ music from a radio in the yard drifted in and out of earshot: *"welcome to the Hotel California....they're living it up at the Hotel California..."*

There is nothing odd in hearing a radio playing snatches of a cheesy 1970's pop song. But there certainly is something pretty damned odd about hearing that particular song in that particular location if you bear in mind that I was here in Somerset to research the life of my great-aunt, a woman who experienced such a life-altering religious revelation in California that she then spent much of her life living there as a nun in a Los Angeles Hindu temple.

I felt slightly unnerved by this coincidental soundtrack and, although a sceptic when it comes to mystical mumbo-jumbo, have to admit that I found myself contemplating that someone of a more religious inclination might imagine the power of karma emanating across the ether, or whatever it does, encouraging me to get on with my researches into the improbable life of a remarkable woman, who certainly did "live it up", and not just in California.

The woman in question was my great-aunt, born Ella Sully in rural Somerset over a hundred years ago, one of ten daughters of a poor agricultural labourer. Partly through luck, but also through sheer energy and force of personality, by the time she died eighty four years later, the girl who started life in such poor circumstances had become Amiya, Dowager Countess of Sandwich. The years in between this transformation were spent in a bizarre and apparently disconnected setting ~ before her improbable marriage into the English aristocracy, Ella spent over twenty years as a religious devotee and nun at a Hindu temple in Los Angeles, California becoming the friend of writers, film stars, artists and poets.

As an old friend of mine, an ex-Fleet Street journalist, said when I outlined her strange story to him ~ "It's got everything! Rags to riches, religion, sex, the English aristocracy, Hollywood, money, court battles ~ what are you waiting for, why don't you write a book ? Christ, I wish I was younger, I'd write it myself." He died less than two weeks later at the age of ninety two. I decided to take his advice and have finally managed to produce this short biography.

Prologue

When I was a small child in the late 1950s & early 60s, on two or three Sundays each year, our family ~ Mum, Dad and three (later four) girls would visit my maternal grandmother who worked as live-in cook and housekeeper to a wealthy widow living in a grand house in Buckinghamshire. We'd drive from Gravesend up the A2 right across London and arrive a couple of hours or so later at Loxborough House at Bledlow Ridge just outside High Wycombe. I loved that journey. It was in the days long before the M25 had been built and we went up the old A2 across Blackheath, through New Cross and Lambeth, over Vauxhall Bridge and then westwards, via Chelsea, out of London towards High Wycombe. Driving back home again in the dark was even better. London in bright lights was a fascinating glimpse of a different world.

Loxborough House was a substantial grey stone Georgian house, set back from the road, approached by a gravel drive and standing in its own grounds. To a small girl, used to an average three-bedroomed semi, it was a strange and slightly forbidding place. The black & white tiled hall, stuffed dead fox's heads displayed on the walls, high panelled doors with crystal handles almost too high to reach and impossible for small hands to turn, and a collection of oriental lacquered boxes, ornaments and ceramics. There were numerous upstairs rooms, some of which opened one into another, which we reached via a small servants' staircase concealed behind a door in the corner of my grandmother's small living room. We were allowed to play in the large gardens at the back of the house and in the grounds beyond, French windows in the main part of the house opened onto a lawn beyond which sheep grazed. These were kept from wandering into the garden by what I now know to be a ha-ha, but which my childish eyes then imagined to be an ancient dried-up castle moat.

During our visits my sisters and I would be ushered into a large drawing room, containing a grand piano, an impressive collection of ornaments, antique furniture and gold-framed oil paintings ~ here we were presented to my grandmother's employer, Mrs. Samuel, the owner of the house. Dorothy Samuel, we were told, had something to do with the Shell oil company and had spent much of her earlier life in the Far East where her late husband had either been a diplomat or conducting the family business, hence the collection of artefacts from China or Japan, or possibly both. A tiny grey-haired woman dressed in black, well-spoken and formal in manner, Mrs. Samuel would attempt to entertain us for half an hour or so with Victorian parlour games and pieces of crystalized ginger. We were on best behaviour and so dutifully played and politely ate the delicacies, but I can only recall feeling ill at ease in her presence, although I'm sure she meant kindly. We were always relieved to get back to the familiarity of the servants quarters where our grandmother, Violet and her second husband, Harry Chart, the chauffeur and general handyman and their young son, Peter, lived. Peter was twenty years younger than his half-sister, Nancy, our mother, and not much older than us girls, his nieces.

During one of these visits, when I was about seven or eight years old, we three little girls were introduced to one of my grandmother's numerous sisters, Amiya who also happened to be visiting. She was, we were told, the Countess of Sandwich. On hearing this startling information one of us apparently enquired, to much adult hilarity, whether we would have to curtsey to her. Of course, we didn't.

Amiya duly appeared, she was by then in her early sixties but still a glamorous figure, expensively dressed, perfumed and made up to the nines. She was a cheerful, lively woman with a cigarette in one hand and glass of booze in the other and she brought with her a reel-to-reel tape recorder which in those days was a piece of expensive technology and something we'd never come across before. Amiya and the adults urged the children to speak into the microphone but my recollection is of being too shy to say a word, intimidated by both the machine itself and the attention of several grown-ups. My mother gamely chatted into it, but when the recording was replayed, I remember feeling confused and slightly anxious because her recorded voice did not sound like my mother at all.

The tape recorder came full circle, so to speak, when nearly fifty years years later my American second cousin, Anne, sent me a box of about thirty small reel-to-reel tapes. These had been recorded in London in the 1960s by Amiya and sent as talking letters to her sister Joy living in California ~ more of these later.

These were days when drink-driving was neither criminalised nor frowned upon and that evening Amiya, despite, according to my mother, having consumed about a bottle of gin, drove herself home from High Wycombe to London in her Bentley. As I was later to find out, she was a legendary drinker. *1. (see notes)

That is the only time I met Amiya. I regret the fact that although she lived for many more years and died when I was aged almost thirty, I never saw her again. To write the story of her life I have had to rely on the official records and the reminiscences of those who did know her and were willing to share what they knew. Most of those who knew her well are now dead, but fortunately some of Amiya's contemporaries, friends and family were very helpful in sharing their memories, letters and photographs. There is also a significant amount in the public record and court and press reports of the time, and I have gleaned much from these.

I have tried to give an objective account of her life, which was stranger than fiction, and her character ~ full of contradictions. She was no saint and didn't pretend to be, but the worst than anyone had to say about her was that sometimes maybe she talked and drank too much and could be rather loud and bossy. All the other evidence appears to shows a kind-hearted, gregarious woman with a huge capacity to enjoy herself and make the most of life; open-minded, generous to a fault, loyal and self-aware. Someone of invincible self-confidence and energy who, through her own determination, threw off the hum-drum life which should have been the lot of a woman of her background and education, and instead seized her chances to live an extraordinary life.

I hope I've done Amiya justice in this short biography.

The Amiya Tapes

During my researches into Amiya's life, I had the good fortune to make contact with several of my mother's distant cousins and second-cousins, most of whom she had never met.

They were the most friendly and helpful individuals and the source of many anecdotes and snippets of family history which have been invaluable and without their contributions I would have had a nigh on impossible task in piecing together Amiya's life.

The most brilliant and unexpected insight into her character and her relationship with her sisters came when I was sent a box of old letter tapes from her American great-niece, Ann Palmerton, the granddaughter of Amiya's elder sister, Joy. These thirty or so reel-to-reel tapes were recorded in the 1960s, mostly in Amiya's West London flat, and sent to Joy who was still living in California after leaving England in the 1920s.

I spent many hours listening to and roughly transcribing the conversations on the tapes, Amiya was rarely alone and mostly in the company of one or more of her sisters, who visited regularly, particularly Sally, who lived in nearby Chelsea and Floss, who lived in Wimbledon.

On several tapes, she was joined by various friends, especially young men, from the Dolce Vita and other fashionable night clubs. Drink was invariably taken, sometimes wine or champagne which Amiya assures Joy is "not hard liquor" sometimes gin and brandy; the clicking of Amiya's cigarette lighter followed by the deep inhalation of smoke was a constant punctuation to the flow of lively conversation. Amiya often cooks meals for her sisters which are the subject of enthusiastic description and praise; they recount the stuff of their lives to Joy, news of children and grandchildren, the odd reminiscences of their mother and their childhood. Occasionally there is a tantalising mention of the bitter feud and court battle between Amiya and her step-children over George Montagu's will.

The overwhelming impression is of warm and close relationship between the sisters, they frequently dissolve into laughter at their own follies or some shared joke and often end up singing, especially after a drink or two.

At first I felt like an eavesdropper on long-forgotten private conversations never intended to be heard by anyone other than Joy, and in a sense that is what I was. But, apart from reading her few religious essays and personal letters, this was the nearest I would ever get to understanding something about who Amiya was, and the tapes certainly made absorbing listening.

There is something poignant about listening to the recorded chatter of people now long dead, the sisters enjoying each other's company in such a genuinely affectionate and uninhibited way.

The tapes reveal Amiya as a lively and talkative woman, often dominating the conversation yet witty and confident enough to be self-deprecating at times, enjoying to the full all the material trappings which her wealth as Dowager Countess of Sandwich had brought ~ the expensive clothes, parties, night clubs, trips to the opera. She talks of buying and selling antiques, spending weekends at her cottage in Berkshire, yet sometimes she also talks earnestly about her religious conviction and the advice of her guru, still at the Los Angeles vedanta. Obviously generous to a fault, she is sometimes taken to task by her sisters for giving away money to people who take financial advantage of her, Amiya invariably responds with her cheery catch-phrase "what the hell !" and a throaty gin and cigarette laugh.

One bit of conversation that sticks with me and neatly encapsulates several aspects of Amiya's life at that time and her personality goes as follows ~ she says:

"We're all going to the Dolce Vita tonight, Susan and Peter, Johnny, Keith and Father Dunn, who's a priest. Carado, the manager, has promised us pink champagne and I've got to perform "The Keys of Heaven" which has become quite a thing, it's a bit of nonsense where I sing and I can't sing but I don't care and everyone laughs and I don't care if they're laughing with me or at me because the thing is people don't laugh enough in this world, so what the hell!"

Chapter One

1902-1915
"We may be poor, but we can at least be clean."

Ella Lilian Sully was born on 28th January 1902 in Hoccombe, a hamlet near the village of Fitzhead in the parish of Lydeard St Lawrence, Somerset. She was the seventh daughter of George and Alice Mary Sully, who went on to produce four more girls, a total of ten surviving daughters, the second-born having died in early infancy. Four boys born to the couple were either still-born or survived for only a few days. Ella's birth certificate shows that a month later her mother travelled the few miles to the town of Taunton to register her new daughter's birth. It's interesting to speculate on what Alice Sully's reaction would have been had she been told that her new baby, daughter of a poor farm labourer would, fifty years later, become the Countess of Sandwich....

Ella was baptised at the age of three months at the church of St. James the Great in Fitzhead, the parish register records her father's occupation as "labourer". At the time of Ella's arrival her mother was thirty two years old and her father thirty six. George Sully spent all his working life as an agricultural labourer and carter on farms around the foot of the Quantock Hills near his birthplace of North Petherton in Somerset, England, he never earned more than fourteen shillings a week. Alice Routley was eighteen when she married George, who was four years her senior, at the parish church of St. Andrew in Wiveliscombe, Somerset on October 9th 1889. Family legend maintained that she eloped with him after her parents had opposed the match because of George Sully's social inferiority to the Routleys and, such was their disapproval, that following the marriage Alice was forbidden any further contact with them.
  Whether this melodramatic version of events is entirely true is questionable: the verifiable facts suggest a rather different situation ~ Alice's birth certificate describes her father, William Routley, as a "labourer", exactly the same class as George Sully, not, on the face of it, a cut above him. The records also show that

William Routley died some months before the marriage and supposed elopement. A decade after their marriage, the 1901 census reveals that, for one night at least, Alice's six year old nephew, John Routley, was staying with her, George and their five daughters. Thirteen years later, George and Alice's eldest daughter, Ada, aged twelve, was sent to live with Alice's mother, Emma Routley. All this suggests that, far from disowning Alice , her mother and at least one of her siblings were on good terms with her. Perhaps any hostility towards George came only from Alice's father and died with him, perhaps the years had softened Emma's own hostility… or perhaps the whole story was largely a concoction. As all the protagonists and their children are long gone, all we have to go on are the verbal accounts handed down through three generations and, like many well-rehearsed family stories, the most likely explanation is that a nugget of truth has been overlaid with a few layers of romantic gloss and exaggeration.

Whatever the truth of the situation, once Alice was married to George there is no doubt that her life from then on was one of hard labour in all senses of the word ~ at least fifteen pregnancies, moving from one tied cottage to another as George's work took him from farm to farm and a constant struggle to feed and clothe the children.

Villages in Somerset where the Sullys lived included Thurloxton, St. Michael Creech, Lydeard St. Lawrence, Hunton and North Petherton; the nearest large town was Taunton. Throughout her married life, Alice's world was physically limited to one of several tiny villages, all within a few miles of each other, bounded by the distance she could walk or to which she might be able to share a lift on a horse-drawn cart.

Alice would have had no time for idle pursuits or hobbies, every waking hour was filled with the relentless grind of providing and caring for a large family. Cooking, cleaning, making and mending clothes plus the weekly backbreaking task of doing the laundry by hand, perhaps growing a few vegetables in the garden. As if that wasn't enough, in order to supplement George's low wages Alice walked the two & a half miles to her sister-in-law's twice a week to earn a few pence by helping Annie, George's sister, with the laundry that she took in from the more well-to-do of the locality. All this with no electricity or gas, no running water and no washing machine or bathroom, not even a flush toilet ~ just an outdoor privy.

Alice also earned a few pennies by sometimes acting as wet-nurse to other women unable to breastfeed their own babies and she also was called upon to stand in as midwife to other women in the village.

But from the recollections of her daughters it seems that despite the poverty of her married life and lowly social status, Alice aspired to Victorian notions of gentility and attempted, with some success, to instil these values into her daughters.

In her old age Florence, the sixth daughter, born in 1900 and Ella's elder by two years, wrote some lively sketches of childhood in the Sully household, these recollections were edited by her daughter, Mary Toase, into a short biography: "Flaxen Hair and Red Pinafores ~ random memories of a country childhood" which gives a vivid insight into the general conditions of agricultural workers' families in England over a hundred years ago; it also recounts the particular dynamics of the Sully family and Ella's place in it. Florence recalled:

"Our home was always far too small for comfort, but somehow we managed. We lived in the kitchen and ate round a well-scrubbed wooden table...... the flagstone floors were covered with brightly coloured rugs made by Mother and the older girls from pieces of sacking into which they threaded coloured rags, with the aid of a wooden skewer. The bedroom floors were plain wood, well-scrubbed. There were only two bedrooms; one for our parents and the newborn baby and the other for the rest of us, with just one large bed. But this bed could be transformed at will into a boat or a mansion; it was the site of our imagination and a wonderful world could be woven into it."

Floss's memoirs depict a close and happy family who lived in very basic conditions on a tiny income, she cheerfully recounts the harsh reality of existence on a diet consisting mainly of watered-down milk and bread and lard, sleeping several children to a bed, walking miles to school in ill-fitting boots and of often being hungry. Floss remembers her mother frequently sitting away from the table at mealtimes, feigning lack of appetite because there was not enough food to go round:

"We were always hungry! Frequently, pangs of hunger drove us to override our consciences, and we regularly stole turnips and swedes from neighbouring farms, peeling them with a tin lid and eating them raw on the way to school."

The adults had to be tough and stoical ~ enduring harsh privations and the constant effort of hard physical work was a daily fact of life. In some ways it had more in common with the medieval world than 21st century Britain ~ no welfare state, a world where church-going and deference to authority were the norm, where strict codes of behaviour and very different roles were set out for women and men, not least because of the lack of effective birth control. Accordingly, George Sully is rarely mentioned by his daughter and then only as a distant figure, a man whose disposition "contrasted violently" to that of the "intelligent and gentle" Alice.

Florence continues:

"As children, we accepted Mother as the provider of food, love and understanding, with Father very much in the background as a rather awesome figure and one who had to be obeyed at all times. We never questioned his authority. However, he was handsome and strong and we have always believed theirs was a happy marriage.

Florence recalled the girls being sometimes entrusted with fourpence halfpenny by their father to go to the pub and buy him an ounce of Bigg's Black Tobacco. During harvest time the men, including George would be given extra cider, which made him merry enough to play the Jew's harp, much to his daughters' great enjoyment. But it was their mother who was the dominant figure in their lives:

Mother's personality was a strong influence on all her girls. She was fiercely loyal, stoical, compassionate and uncomplaining all her life. She remained devoted to our father, despite all his shortcomings, accepting as her lot that our upbringing was her responsibility, and hers alone. Father rarely saw us; Mother would hustle us up to bed before he arrived home for his tea. She had the good sense, for the sake of marital harmony, to pack us off upstairs in the evenings – half past five in winter, an hour later in summer"

Being sent to bed so early meant the girls had plenty of time to play upstairs in the bedroom they all shared. Oddly enough, given the destiny of one of the little girls, a favourite game was recalled by Florence as follows:

"We lived in a world of make-believe ~ we would sit on the floor around the large bed (which they all shared) and pretend to be 'gentry' eating sumptuous dinners off priceless china."

Years later, as middle-aged women, some of the sisters would gather in Amiya's London flat and the conversation would occasionally turn to their childhood and their parents. They would stamp on the floor in unison and call out "Stir your stumps!" in imitation of their mother's favourite mannerism and rallying cry. Amiya later remembered her father calling her "the left-handed skivvy" for her dexterity in slicing a loaf of bread very thinly, which must have been a useful skill with so many mouths to feed. Sally (as Winifred,the eighth sister, was called in adulthood) recalls their father telling off the teenage Ella, who was home on a visit, for wearing a dress he described as being so low-cut "everyone can see your stocking tops down the front of it". References to Alice administering "a good hiding" on occasion to her naughty little girls might sound shocking to modern ears but a hundred years ago physical punishment of both children and adults was considered necessary and right. Ella is described by Florence as *very imaginative and creative, but always needed to be the centre of attraction."* A polite way, maybe, of saying her sister was a bit of a show-off which suggests that, even as a child, Ella was not lacking in confidence.

Conditions were always overcrowded, there were only ever two bedrooms in these tiny cottages ~ one for the parents and youngest baby, the other for the rest of the girls, always sharing just one or two beds.

The Sully girls all looked alike, blue-eyed and with long fair hair, rigorously combed and worn in tight plaits during the week to avoid catching head lice from "dirty children" at school, then washed on Saturdays, plaited and left overnight so that on Sundays, when worn loose, the girls' hair would appear all wavy. "Such vanity!" as Florence recalled. She also described how the Sully girls were dressed identically in red pinafores all week with white for Sundays, and "Summer & winter alike, we wore thick black woollen stockings, knitted by Mother, and hobnailed boots."

Despite their cramped and poor living conditions, their mother was a stickler for cleanliness, her motto being: "We may be poor, but we can at least be clean." Her daughters, on their return from school, were subjected to "a good scrubbing down by mother or an older sister."

The Sullys, like most Edwardian families, kept the Sabbath holy. The girls were forbidden many activities, including sewing because, so they were told, this would have meant putting a needle into the body of Christ. Twice every Sunday the girls and their mother went to the Wesleyan Chapel, but later in life they could not recall their father ever attending.

"Each girl would fight for the honour of walking with Mother and holding her hand. We were so proud of her, in her beautiful black bonnet, velvet beaded waist-length cape and rustling skirt. This fine attire was probably her trousseau, or clothes she wore before her marriage; they were far finer than anything she was able to afford later."

Sometimes they would go to a tiny Bethel Methodist chapel, Methodists had no priests but lay preachers, ordinary working men who would deliver long sermons in the Somerset vernacular; Florence remembers the sisters giggling uncontrollably as one such preacher:

"ranted and raved about Hellfire, banging his fist down hard on the pulpit, until at last he finished, utterly spent. He would then mop his brow and exclaim "I be all of a shake, I be!"

The girls attended Sunday School, choir practice and joined the Band of Hope where

"even as young children we were forced to sign The Pledge:
I promise here by Grace divine
to drink no spirits, ale, or wine
nor will I buy or sell or give
strong drink to others while I live
for my own good this Pledge I take
but also for my neighbours' sake
and this my strong resolve shall be
No drink, no drink, no drink for me
'I, the undersigned, do agree that I will not use intoxicating liquors as a beverage'.

Most of the Sully sisters were to break the Pledge in adult life, but none in quite such determined and flamboyant style as Ella.

Betty Steele, daughter of the eldest Sully sister, Ada, writing many years later to a cousin, related the following anecdote involving Alice and the local Anglican vicar:

"Three of the boys (George & Alice's sons) were still-born and the fourth only lived for a week. Thereby hangs a tale:- the local Church of England parson called while the baby was still hanging on to life and said that he should be

christened or he would not be allowed into the Kingdom of Heaven. Grandma's answer was "Get out!" She told the parson the baby had never had the chance to do wrong and she was not going to have him pulled about in his last hours and that the baby had a greater chance of Heaven than he (the parson) had as he'd lived longer and done more wrong; hence the reason why the family went to the Methodist church from then on."

Betty went on to recount:

"Auntie Doris (the seventh sister) once asked her mother why she had so many children and her answer was - 'They are a natural outcome when you love someone.' What a simple answer, bless her dear heart."

In the few written and spoken records that remain, all the sisters show love for their mother and an appreciation of how she worked so hard to bring them up, Alice seems to have set them a shining example of good motherhood. Years later Ella herself wrote of Alice as " the wisest of all mothers" and spoke of her as "the most wonderful woman in the world", this latter remark was made after a few drinks but the sentiment remains.

The girls were born over a period of twenty years and so by the time the younger ones were born, the older sisters had already left home and were working or married. The strangest thing is that the ten sisters never in their lives all met together. Maybe not so strange, though, if you consider that the girls left school at twelve or thirteen to start work, often in some sort of domestic service, which meant living away from home. Eventually five of them lived abroad at various times in the days when travel was neither easy nor cheap.

Another strange family arrangement, to modern eyes at least, was that some time after her birth in 1908, the second youngest Sully daughter, Violet, was adopted by George's younger brother, Thomas and his wife, also named Alice. Violet was taken to live with them in Merthyr Tydfil, South Wales. Some years before, the unemployed Thomas had walked from north Somerset to the south Wales coalfields in search of work. There he found a job as a miner in a colliery in Merthyr and married a local woman, Alice Yorath. Soon after the marriage, Thomas was badly injured in a pit accident and remained a semi-invalid for the rest of his life, possibly as a consequence of this Thomas and Alice had no children of their own.

It is not known whether George and Alice's decision to give Violet away was made before or after her birth, although it seems very unlikely that had she been a boy it would have happened. But the arrival of yet another girl must have set the seal on things and in many ways it would have been a practical solution to two problems: removing yet another child from the hard-pressed George and Alice and giving the blessing of a new baby to the childless Thomas and Alice. A benefit then to all concerned, apart sadly for poor Violet herself who endured a harsh and lonely upbringing as an only child under the cold and strictly religious Alice; Violet later referred to her adoptive mother as "the hardest woman I ever knew," and was not told of her biological parents and nine sisters until her sixteenth birthday, and she did not actually meet them until some time after receiving this shocking news. In 1926, at the age of eighteen, Violet left Wales for London to train as a nurse.

Florence said later that neither she nor the rest of her sisters knew anything about what she termed "this extra sister." Yet considering that at the time of Violet's birth, Florence was nearly nine years old and the elder sisters ranged in age up to eighteen years old, it is difficult to understand how the older girls would have been unaware of her arrival and subsequent removal to Wales.

Another thing that doesn't tally is that although the accepted family version of events is that Violet was adopted very soon after birth, in fact, she is listed in the 1911 census, aged two, as living in Somerset with George & Alice and seven of the other girls. So she was not a newborn baby but rather a toddler of at least two years old, when she was sent to Wales; even stranger therefore that her older sisters did not appear to recall her existence.

One obvious possibility is that in fact George and Alice were not Violet's parents at all, but her grandparents, and that she was the illegitimate child of their eldest daughter. Ada, who had left home at the age of 14 to work in a hotel in Taunton and would have been aged 18 at the time of Violet's birth. It was not uncommon in those days for a mother of childbearing age to effectively shield her unmarried daughter from the social shame of giving birth by claiming an illegitimate grandchild as her own son or daughter. Even better, in terms of out of sight out of mind perhaps, if the child could be sent a good distance away to another close family member who could be relied on not to reveal the origin of the child. There is no real evidence to support this speculation, just a possibility, given the ages of those involved and a few tantalising hints that maybe all was not as it seemed ~

Florence wrote this curious piece of information about Ada: *"when still very young, she married Frank Spicer, a secret she kept from the family for some time, while wearing her wedding ring round her neck."* What prompted Ada to keep her marriage a secret from her family? Was she worried that to tell them before the wedding would have risked someone revealing to an unwitting Frank that she had borne an illegitimate baby?

Violet's birth certificate names her parents as George and Alice Sully, the informant of the birth was Alice who, for whatever reason, did not register the birth until more than six weeks later. Such a long delay was actually in breach of the legal requirement to register a child within 42 days of birth and while this may have been due to mundane reasons, could it have been that Alice, if she was not the baby's mother, was wrestling with her conscience over giving false information about Violet's parentage to the registrar?
We do know that Alice was "fiercely loyal" to her family, a strong and decisive woman who hadn't hesitated to order a hectoring vicar out of her home, it doesn't seem out of character that, in order to help her eldest daughter, she might well have been prepared to claim this baby was her own.

And was Violet's harsh upbringing perhaps a reflection of the strict chapel-going Alice Yorath's judgemental and uncompromising attitude towards a child born in sin? Who knows.

In all likelihood Violet really was the daughter of Alice and George and everything which might seem a bit questionable about her birth and childhood can just as easily be explained by human error, lapses of memory or downright odd behaviour by some of those involved, but there still does remain a question mark over her place in the family.

Chapter Two

1915-1930
"Put *can't* in your pocket and take out try."

Because of their poor circumstances all the Sully girls had to leave school and start work at the age of twelve or thirteen in order to contribute to the family income. And so, in 1915, Ella began her first job as a shop assistant in the rough dockside area of Bristol; no doubt she quickly learnt a rather different pace and type of life than the quiet rural backwater of home in the village. She worked in the Bristol shop until the age of fifteen, when she went to work as a domestic servant in a farmhouse just outside the city.

An anecdote about the teenage Ella related by one of her sisters gives a hint of the reckless self-confidence that would become a hallmark of her later life. The story goes like this: Ella had saved the money to have her photograph taken in a studio on her day off and, unknown to the lady of the house, had "borrowed" from her a necklace to wear for the occasion. The photograph was produced, the necklace returned to its jewellery box and Ella, delighted with the result, was on the brink of showing it around the household only to realise that if she did so and her employer got to hear of her own jewellery adorning the neck of the maid, she would probably lose her job and good reference. Ella herself laughed at her own lack of foresight and probably enjoyed showing off the photo to her sisters and relating the story of her own boldness.

Aged eighteen, Ella moved to Bath where she lived at 3, Henry Street although it is not known where she worked. In February 1921, three weeks after her nineteenth birthday, at the now demolished St James' Church in Great Orchard Street, she married twenty eight year old Seymour Douglas Besant Corbin, known as Jack, the son of a hotel proprietor, described on their marriage certificate as a " piano expert" living at West's Hotel in Bath. The official witnesses were, slightly oddly, two individuals with Germanic-sounding surnames: E P Lenenbeyer and C P Engler. They were probably friends of the couple, but it is unusual that neither was a member of the Sully family; Ella's father, in particular, would normally have been expected to be witness at his daughter's wedding. Did her parents, perhaps, disapprove of Jack Corbin? Did they even know of the wedding? After all, their eldest daughter, Ada, had only told them of her marriage to Frank Spicer several weeks after the event, so there was something of a track record of secret Sully weddings.

In any case, Ella and Jack's marriage was short-lived and the couple went their separate ways after only a year or so. It's impossible to second guess what went wrong between them, but twenty years later Ella, by then known as Amiya, admitted to her friend Christopher Isherwood that as a girl she had been 'vain and silly' and that the separation from Jack Corbin had been for insufficient reasons and resulted from a fit of pique on her part.

Following the collapse of the marriage Ella moved to London where, in 1923, she began a series of jobs in up-market dress shops. This suggests that Ella was already smoothing out any rough country edges to her speech and manners and aspiring to an occupation involving contact with, if not entry to, a different class of society. But, according to Floss, she "never really settled". She was, however, "always well-dressed and would spend her last penny on clothes, even if it meant no dinner", which it apparently frequently did. Floss ~ now married and also living in London ~ describes visiting Ella and finding her "near starvation" and having to exchange with her sister last year's hat or skirt for the occasional square meal.

By 1929 Ella had formed a relationship which, nearly thirty years later, she herself coyly described as "an attachment which could not easily have been broken" and that as the months passed "my attachment grew stronger until in the early Spring of 1930, when it was inexorably broken by death. My life was made void: I was left empty and alone." * See Note 1

It can only be assumed that she was, in a rather flowery way, describing a love affair in London several years after the collapse of her marriage to Jack Corbin.

Just at this point in her life, Ella's older sister, Ivy (but always known in adult life as Joy owing to a misreading of her name by an employer), who had been living in the USA, returned to England for a visit. In her teens, Joy had contracted TB and spent some time in a sanatorium in Somerset; when she had recovered she was employed as a nanny or maid by Dr. Alexander Irvine and when he and his family moved to California in the 1920s, Joy went with them. Here, after a time, she took up dressmaking and after a few years was able to set up her own business which, according to Ella, involved "creating and making beautiful feminine luxuries ~ to meet the wants, rather than the needs, of the rich."

In 1925 Joy married an American artist, Donald Palmerton, and the following year, their only child, a son, Calson, was born. The marriage ended within a couple of years when Joy left Donald, taking Calson with her. She went on to marry twice more. *See Note 2

In 1930, during Joy's visit to England, Ella made the momentous decision to return to California with her sister. With nothing much to keep her in England, she must have felt that America offered her the chance of starting again and she later recalled that:

"From childhood we had been taught by the wisest of mothers never to say 'I can't' but rather 'to put can't in your pocket and take out try'. This homily stood me in good stead..."

She also paid tribute to Joy's "self sacrifice and generosity" in using her own savings to pay for Ella's trans-Atlantic passage. The sisters boarded the Dutch passenger ship, SS Statendam in Southampton on 4th July and set sail the following day bound for New York.

It was this journey, more than anything else, that was to lead to an extraordinary turn of events.

Chapter Three

1930-1952
A stranger in a strange land

Ella and Joy arrived in New York at the end of July 1930 and then travelled across America to Joy's home in San Francisco, California. Within a few months of arriving, Ella was invited, one Sunday morning, by an unnamed male acquaintance to join him in a visit to a Hindu temple on Webster Street. Twenty five years later she described the profound effect that first visit had on her:

*"The words swami, Vedanta, yoga, meditation were totally unknown to me. I had far to go and much to learn. Even so, while I sat there in the stillness I experienced the most extraordinary conviction that I belonged there: and the strange sensation of warmth that enveloped me, I could only describe later, was as if a blanket had been wrapped around me. I had come home. Time has not dimmed this memory, nor will it ever. Already my course was being set, and I was being launched on the path of no return. As I listened to the chanting of those first Vedic prayers that peculiar sensation came over me; my spine tingled and my whole body felt a mass of goose-flesh. I have no clear recollection of the words I heard that morning; I only know that every word made sense. Something within me responded, so much so that, for the duration of my stay in San Francisco I attended every lecture and every class – three times a week." * See Note 1*

Ella's companion to that memorable first visit never accompanied her there again, she only referred to him as "a metaphysical rover" who was always equally ready to sympathise or ridicule, something she sarcastically noted made him "more broad-minded than I". But he had served his purpose in what Ella believed was divine guidance.

But the mundane matter of finding work was proving more elusive than spiritual fulfilment; Ella's main purpose in going to America had been to work in partnership with Joy as a seamstress but the great financial crash of 1929-30 brought an abrupt standstill to Joy's business. Very soon she was no longer able to provide work or accommodation for Ella who recalled:

"I, a stranger in a strange land, was thrown upon my own resources – and how limited they were I was soon to find out."

In October 1931 she moved to Los Angeles, nearly four hundred miles away, in the hope of finding work. Here she rented a one-room apartment and tried to establish herself as an independent seamstress.

One of her first actions on reaching Los Angeles was to contact the Vedanta Centre of Southern California Hollywood whose address she had been given by the Hindu temple in San Francisco.

* See Note 2

One Sunday morning, keen to make a good impression and arrive in time to take part in the rituals, she got off the street-car at the junction of Hollywood Boulevard and Ivar Avenue and set out for the Centre at 1946 Ivar Avenue, unfortunately Ella's eagerness was not matched by her sense of direction and she immediately began walking the wrong way. By the time she realised her mistake, she was already late, it was a hot day and on reaching her destination, a weather-beaten, old green bungalow, Ella remembered

"I was almost sobbing for want of breath. My teeth were on edge, my heart was pounding and I was soaked with the sweat of my hurrying. Little did I know then that I was standing on the threshold of what was to become my home for the next twenty years."

For the next few weeks she attended every lecture and class given by Prabhavananda, the Swami in charge of the Centre.

Meanwhile, the attempt to earn a living as a seamstress was foundering. Despite over a year spent doing the job, by her own admission Ella had neither the training, skill or patience for the profession, she later described her ham-fisted attempts at dressmaking: ending up with garments stitched inside out and having to unpick and re-stitch almost every attempt. After losing her first client things only got worse and, after paying the rent for the apartment and for the hire of the sewing machine which gave her so much trouble, there was often little or no money left, even for food.

It was now 1933 and things were at a low ebb, even if she had wanted to return to England, there was no money for a ticket home. She had no choice but to get on with things as they were and despite feeling lonely, she persevered with her studies at the Centre and took increasing comfort from them, finding that:

"The meaning of Vedanta was fast taking hold of my mind and heart. In it I found hope and a lessening of the loneliness which conditions had imposed upon me."

After a time she accepted an invitation from Swami Prabhavananda for a private appointment with him.....

"How kind he was. How patiently he listened to the feeble and inconsequential tale I unfolded while, all the time, I picked nervously at the wicker tub-shaped chair I sat in. I needed a friend rather than a spiritual guide, or so I thought. But how often since I have cringed with shame at my audacity in imposing upon that holy man my stupid little problems. But they were very real and I was very lonely."

Ella was introduced to Sister Lalita, an American woman aged seventy two, born Carrie Mead Wyckoff, who had been a devotee in the Vedanta Society for many years. She had given her home at 1946 Ivar Avenue to the Society, hence its' use as a centre/temple. Ella saw Lalita as a shining example of selfless devotion and service and would later try to emulate the older woman's obedience and patience, with varying degrees of success.

Ella was soon invited to share meals with Prabhavananda and Lalita, she felt they did this partly out of knowledge of her financial predicament but was nevertheless taken by surprise when the pair suggested that she should give up her precarious way of life as a seamstress; their plan was that Ella should move into the house next door to the Vedanta Centre which was owned by Lalita's sister who, in three weeks time was to be left alone when her daughter married and moved away. Ella would act as paid helper to Lalita's ageing sister and also as assistant at the Centre. Ella was delighted at the suggestion and moved out of her apartment and stayed at the Centre acting as a volunteer helper for the three weeks prior to the anticipated final move next door. But at the last minute Lalita's sister & niece had a change of plan and decided that Ella's services were not now required. She was bitterly disappointed at losing this chance for paid employment which would also have allowed her to continue her unpaid work at the Centre. When Prabhavananda asked her to stay on, unpaid, at the Centre but with free board and lodging, at first Ella was sorely tempted by the offer but then, what she described as her "British pride and stubbornness" prevented her from accepting what she interpreted as charity. She became determined to find some way of supporting herself and very soon an opportunity presented itself.

In 1934, through one of the Swami's students, Ella learned that a French actress, who had recently enjoyed stage and film success in Europe, was recently arrived in Beverley Hills and looking for an assistant to help her with English pronunciation and grammar. She specified that this assistant should be English, not American. This was enough for Ella who, despite her complete lack of qualifications, seized her chance ~ she bought a new hat and paid the actress a visit to offer her services. The meeting went well and she was offered the job which was well-paid and involved spending three months living with the actress and her entourage in a house on the California coast.

The actress was Suzanne Georgette Charpentier, a few years younger than Ella, who went by the stage name Annabella. She was currently being publicised in Hollywood as "Continental Film Star Number One." In 1926, at the age of sixteen, Annabella had made her screen debut in Abel Gance's film Napoleon and soon became the protégée of the director Rene Clair. When Annabella first arrived in Hollywood, she had been met at the airport by fellow countryman Charles Boyer, with whom she had appeared in the film La Bataille in 1931. The idea was to improve her English skills in order that she could make it as a film actress in Hollywood, and so for three months she underwent an intensive course instructed by Ella, who by her own account:

"Revelled in the luxury of freedom from financial anxiety and enjoyed the companionship which sprang up between my pupil and myself. My task was not easy."

She also recalled the hours spent anxiously burning the midnight oil in order to keep one jump ahead of Annabella, who was blissfully unaware that her teacher was not formally qualified and, in fact, was making things up as she went along. But the combination of Ella's self-confidence, hard work and charm clearly made up for the academic deficit because at the end of the three months, she was offered another contract in voice coaching, this time in New York.

All this time she had kept close contact with the Vedanta Centre and when

Prabhavananda repeated his offer to take up rent-free residence at the Ivar Avenue temple and spend time there in unpaid domestic work and study, Ella was confronted with perhaps the most important decision of her life. On the one hand, New York, financial independence and an exciting life-style amongst the theatrical set; on the other, the Centre and all it stood for. It only took her a short while to decide:

"Money has power and great persuasion but where there is no money, one must depend upon grace and love. I chose the Centre and by so doing lost nothing but gained everything worthwhile."

She was to spend the next twenty years of her life at Ivar Avenue, the early years of which she later looked upon as "the happiest period of my life". It was a simple yet sometimes difficult life. At this point Vedanta was not the fashionable cult of the rich and famous of Hollywood which it later became. Those at the Centre lived from hand to mouth, relying on the good-will offerings of a few staunch devotees, Ella herself divided her time between domestic work and spiritual contemplation. Much of the former involved cooking, Prabhavananda taught her the art of making curry at which she became an expert. "How many tons of curry I made during these years would be difficult to estimate!" she later recalled.

The discipline and self-sacrifice involved in the spiritual side of things did not come easily, she described her "abysmal shame" on recollecting her early impatience with the slow-moving, old Sister Lalita and her initial constant questioning of the severe discipline imposed on her. There was the unremitting requirement to control and subdue personal desires which was an intrinsic part of the religion. Ella later wrote that it was only in retrospect that she understood the purpose and necessity of this, but at the time her "hurt and self-justified ego" complained about what she could only see the "unfairness" of it. But gradually:

"I came to know what peace was. I knew that what I was being taught was true. I knew that the kingdom of God was within, and within the reach of us all. I caught a glimpse of the light shining in the darkness."

When she took up residence at the Centre, Ella was given the Sanskrit name, Amiya, by which from then on she would always be known, even by members of her own family who did not share her new religion. She became an American citizen in 1938 and by this time had no thought of ever returning to England.

The Centre itself was becoming transformed; by the late 1930s it had raised enough money to build a small temple in the garden of 1946 Ivar Avenue. It was an exotic sight, even for Hollywood, a white building with oriental domes and golden turrets.

Joining Amiya & Lalita in the mid-1930s was a third "nun", Helen Kennedy, renamed Sudhira and in 1939 she was followed by Ruth Ingeborg Folling, a seventeen year old High School student given the name Sarada who quickly became the Swami's prize pupil.

Sarada later wrote an account of her days in the Vedanta Society in which she recalled:

"I'd already taken in Amiya's friendliness, her blonde hair, her plumpness and her English accent. I soon gathered that she managed the household. She had prepared the first of my numberless meals of "dhal bhat" with curries of chicken, lamb and fish. Before each of our meals we chanted in chorus our Grace mantra. We repeated this mantra in Sanskrit but I'm sure we all knew the English translation. I came each day by bus to Hollywood. It was a good climb up the hill to reach the Temple tucked away in the Hollywood hills. It was almost obscured in a residential area. I was given the pleasant task of picking flowers for the daily puja. Sudhira instructed me as to the number of flowers required, plus a few three pronged blades of grass. I learned how to make the fragrant sandalwood-paste by rubbing pieces of the wood on a pumice stone with a little water. After finishing our meal, served promptly at 1:15, my job was to wash the dishes. I remained for the evening Vespers, experiencing this as a lovely ceremony of the "waving of the lights", chanting and quiet meditation. One day and without a "by your leave" I didn't go home. No one was surprised, but rather they were pleased. I bedded down in a corner of Amiya's room in the old green cottage. I soon learned to both cook and clean through the patient guidance of Amiya and Sudhira. At that time joining a Hindu religious group, thought certainly to be a cult, was hardly the "in" thing to do, even though the Vedanta philosophy seriously interested a number of intellectuals including Aldous Huxley, Christopher Isherwood, Somerset Maugham and others. At the time I hadn't even heard of them! One of the exciting events we experienced was the day that Chris (Isherwood) managed to have Greta Garbo come for lunch." *See Note 3*

Increasingly the Centre was attracting artists, writers and actors and young people who felt drawn by this exotic religion and so the number of nuns and monks and hangers-on increased. The place was not a monastery in the usual sense of the word, its inhabitants were granted permission to come and go or stay away overnight if they wished, it offered a kind of religious bohemianism and oriental laissez-faire which appealed to a section of the Hollywood elite.

In 1943 a regular visitor and student was Christopher Isherwood, the English writer who had emigrated to the USA three years before. His diaries give a frank account of life at "the Swamitage", as the Centre became known amongst the worldly glitterati who now embraced Vedanta. Isherwood's waspish observations of the rivalries between the devotees contrast with Amiya's rather more veiled and often sentimental recollections.

An astute and brutally honest commentator, Isherwood was typically forthright in his remarks about Amiya, who would become his close friend for over forty years.
He gives his impressions of her when they first met, when she was aged thirty nine:

"Amiya was a big blonde woman who must have been very pretty but was now running to fat. A marvellous cook and a born manager, she was jealous and bossy. She said bitter things which she immediately regretted.

She adored the Swami (Prabhavananda) and was terribly possessive: she hated anyone else to wait on him: she wanted to be undisputed mistress of the household. The Swami knew this and scolded her unmercifully, often humiliating her to tears in public. At first this shocked me, Then I began to see how necessary it was for her to be forced to submit – even to occasional injustice. As a girl she had been vain, silly, spoilt, as she now admitted. Now she was achieving, painfully, a kind of greatness. She was warm-hearted, passionately loyal, absolutely sincere, tactless, emotional, rude; the prototype of Martha in the gospels." * See Note 4

In the opening chapters of the autobiographical 'My Guru and his Disciple' Isherwood describes life at the Centre in the 1940s as a kind of family where the generations lived together, everyone on top of everyone else: there was no privacy and there were no secrets. The communal meals were vegetarian and, surprisingly for the time, men were expected to help with the washing up. Everything out in the open and everyone encouraged to speak his or her mind. Visitors were always welcome, as a few more or less could easily be catered for and tended to make things more exciting.

This impression is also backed up by John Yale, a devotee who joined the Centre a few years after Isherwood.

*"Meals were taken irregularly by the inmates; the women wore dressing gowns sometimes till midday; there was no such thing as an office with office hours; the telephone often went unanswered and the mail undistributed; no one hesitated to express his or her temperament. One of the members had organized his room for the production of gourmet meals, accompanied by choice wines which he drew from a supply he had stocked in the Centre's basement." * See Note 5*

Yale, born in 1913, became an initiate in the Ramakrishna Order in 1950 where he took the name Prema Chaitanya, later becoming Swami Vidyatmananda. Originally a successful Chicago publisher he came to know Amiya well and they became friends, corresponding and visiting each other for many years right up to her death. At first, however, there was a distinct personality clash between the two, with Yale at one point complaining to Swami about what he considered to be Amiya's "scandalous behaviour". Yale did not specify the nature of her behaviour but observed, as Isherwood did, that Amiya was finding it difficult to adjust to the influx of young disciples to the Centre in the early 1940s and often felt her senior position in the household threatened by these newcomers.

"The newcomers were younger than Amiya and proved to be more adaptable than she to religious life. Amiya was rajasic she wanted to dress well, to have a good time, to go out. I saw her as a discontented and restless person. Prabhavananda's frequent demands that she should make some strenuous effort to to deepen her spiritual life did not interest her seriously. She possessed the authority of long association with the Swami and the Centre but followed no visible discipline, providing, I felt, a bad example (to new young initiates)..."
See Note 6

Yale recounts how, when he condemned Amiya's behaviour to the Swami, he was severely rebuked and told: "Never judge a situation until you know the end of the story." Yale was later ashamed of his youthful priggish attitude towards Amiya especially when, many years later she wrote to him:

" I wish to make a confession. All those years ago when you first came to the Centre some of us found the things you said shocking. I seriously considered

complaining to Swami about you. I'm glad I didn't. As I have watched your development these three decades and seen what a devotee you have become, I know that such an evaluation would have been hasty and wrong. I'm sorry I ever had such feelings."

Yale said that he "read these lines with burning cheeks."

At this point in the story it's worth mentioning the following piece of family gossip – for years my mother had told us that her aunt (Amiya), while living in America, had had an affair with the film actor, Tyrone Power. Although largely forgotten today, Power was a Hollywood star of the 1930s and 40s. I had taken this information with a large pinch of salt until, while researching Amiya's life, I discovered an interesting coincidence.

In the late 1940s, a film was being made of Somerset Maugham's novel, "The Razor's Edge", this was a story of one man's religious quest and Tyrone Power, recently demobilized after more than three years in the Marine Corps during the War, had been chosen to play Maugham's hero, Larry. Somerset Maugham himself had visited the Vedanta Centre on several occasions and, at his request, Power came to the Ivar Avenue house to discuss with Prabhavananda the characterization of Larry. Swami apparently found it difficult to visualize Tyrone Power, an inveterate womaniser, being able to portray what was known in the Vedanta trade as "a realized soul". But the two talked the matter over, and as a result Power studied the role and its religious implications with care, in an attempt to give as authentic a portrayal as he was capable of giving.

For a time Power was a regular visitor to the Centre, he would almost inevitably have met Amiya who at this time was working as the Swami's Secretary. So, rather than the far-fetched fantasy I had sceptically dismissed, it does seem entirely possible that some kind of affair, however fleeting, could have taken place.

Christopher Isherwood, in his usual forthright way, gives another insight into life at the Vedanta Centre and the tensions which inevitably arose from the close proximity between students, nuns and monks.

In February 1943 one of those who moved into the Centre was seventeen-year-old Webster Milam, a high-school student from Arizona who had decided to become a monk at the tender age of fourteen. His mother was interested in Vedanta and so did not oppose her son living at the Centre. Isherwood described Milam as a square, muscular boy, very hairy and strong as an ox; serious, very obstinate and yet good-natured. Not only good at carpentry and building, he was also a jujitsu champion. By September of that same year, Isherwood was curious as to why Milam was badly slacking in every way, meditating very little, dodging the housework and eating hugely. He then adds that he (Milam) allowed himself to be mothered and practically hand-fed by Amiya, who was getting far too emotionally involved with the teenager. A few weeks later Isherwood feared that the Ivar Avenue Centre was on the verge of eruption, one of the reasons being that Webster Milam's mother had written the Swami a "really poisonous" letter accusing Amiya of having more-than-motherly feelings towards her young son. This letter upset Amiya greatly, so much so that she took to her bed complaining of terrible pains in her legs.

Was there was any substance in Mrs. Milam's accusation? If there wasn't then it's understandable that Amiya would have felt upset at having her platonic concern for the boy being so spitefully misunderstood. If there was substance in the accusation, Amiya certainly wasn't the only person at the Vedanta to take an interest in worldly pleasures and neither was she the worst: according to Isherwood another devotee, Sister Sudhira "caused more trouble at Ivar Avenue than everybody else put together".

Isherwood goes on to relate how despite his own arguments with Amiya and particularly after making things up with her following a row, he "hadn't realised how fond of her I am" and "I must never forget this about her: her longing for affection, her loyalty, her struggle to create a family and a home."

In 1944, a generous donor named Mr. Kellogg (not of Corn Flakes fame), who had made a fortune in linseed oil, gave the Vedanta Society a house and several acres of land in Montecito on the hill sides of Santa Barbara. These new premises provided far more luxurious living conditions for the nuns, including Amiya, who was put in charge of the new premises by Prabhavananda, and moved there from Ivar Avenue.

The new estate, named Ananda Bhavan, was set in a beautiful part of California on a mountain slope, on the edge of national forest land. It had fine views over the bay and its islands.

As Sarada described it, Ananda Bhavan marked a significant change in the living conditions of the devotees, whose religious devotions did not sound too onerous:

"Even our wealthy neighbors did not enjoy a grander view, or eat three tastier meals a day. We each had our own room and bath. Our daily

chores were light, and only once a year the Siva Ratri demanded a small loss of sleep and fasting. Our daily routine pivoted around periods of meditation and work, and performing the daily puja and evening Vespers. Even after we women moved to Santa Barbara there were numerous trips back to Hollywood for Pujas and other events."

A very comfortable life in the California sun compared to the one being lived by most of Amiya's sisters back in cold, grey England where the Second World War was imposing a grim existence of food rationing, the black-out, air raids and anxiety.

Three years later, Amiya took her brahmacharya vows and officially became a nun of the Ramakrishna Order, Sarada recalled:

"In '47 it was as though the place was abuzz with spiritual "vibes" as Swamis from all over the country came to assist in our first Brahmachari vows. At that time we didn't appreciate how hard Swami had pressed the Order to include women both in India and the West. Up till then we had been loosely called "nuns." Amiya and I became Brahmacharinis [similar to novice or postulant] on that revolutionary day."

Isherwood recalls that Amiya was often sparring with the other inhabitants, usually about the management of the Centre which, having been appointed to the task by Swami himself, she felt she knew best how to run. Her combative tendencies even extended to the Centre's wealthy benefactor, the aged Mr. Kellogg who was a regular visitor, and his much younger wife who disapproved of the Vedanta Society and, despite being hugely wealthy herself, grudged her husband's financial generosity towards it. Isherwood described how, after an altercation with the couple, Amiya confided to him her view that young Mrs. Kellogg was unhappy and discontented because she married the old man for his money, assuming he would die soon; but he had lived ten years since then and was still chasing other women. Ironically, events in Amiya's own life a few years later would lead others to make almost exactly the same comments about her.

Life went on at the Hollywood Centre and its' offshoot at Santa Barbara, it was a paradoxical mixture of religious devotion, worldly pleasure, artistic experimentation, self-denial, self-indulgence and the general fall-out resulting from communal living. During the 1940s, Amiya wrote several essays for inclusion in the Society's publications, including one on the marriage of Sarada

Devi, a revered holy woman of the previous century and another on the lesson to be learned from the New Testament story of Martha, the follower of Christ.

It is clear from the recollections of her contemporaries that Amiya's religious devotions were often lacking. According to John Yale, although a close attachment had grown between Amiya and her guru, Prabhavananda, over many years, she remained, as always, "wayward and thoughtless". When she was taken to task by the Swami for neglecting meditation and worship, she invariably repented and promised to reform. But her new starts were short-lived and she continued to be a source of controversy amongst the other devotees.

But in 1952 ,five years after her ordination, the arrival at the Hollywood Centre of a distinguished visitor from England was to have profound consequences for the ever-restless Amiya. The visitor was George Montagu, the ninth Earl of Sandwich, on a stop-over in Los Angles during an ocean cruise from England.

George Charles Montagu was born in 1874 and had inherited his title and estate from his uncle in 1916. He was now a seventy seven year old widower following the death of his wife Alberta a year earlier. Alberta Sturges had been the daughter of William Sturges, a Chicago banker who died when Alberta was aged sixteen; the following year her mother, Elizabeth, married a New York wholesale grocer and millionaire, Francis H Leggett. From then until her marriage to George Montagu in 1905, Alberta spent most of her time in Paris and London where in 1901 she made her society debut. Here her mother was one of the leading hostesses of the rich American colony during the reign of Edward VII.

Alberta Sturges was one of many wealthy young American women who flocked to Europe during this time. From 1870 to the outbreak of World War 1, around 350 US heiresses married into the British aristocracy bringing badly needed large amounts of cash into their husbands' huge estates. At today's values, it's estimated that they brought with them the equivalent of £1 billion of new world wealth.

Alberta's mother, Betty Leggett, was a clever operator who made it her full time work in London to ensure both her daughters met "men of brain and position" in London, she carefully chose the venues and social events most likely to secure "good" marriages for them and her efforts paid off ~ Alberta became the wife of an earl, and her younger daughter married an English viscount, Henry Margesson.

Betty's husband, Frank Leggett remained slightly dubious about the wisdom of what could be seen as marrying for social rank; he wrote to his wife on George and Alberta's engagement: *"I shall try to show as much pride in the connection as you and Alberta must feel, but above all hope that happiness will prove the dominant feature of the whole affair, For happiness is worth more than millions of money and the most exalted positions"*

There's nothing to suggest that Leggett's hopes were not fulfilled, George and Alberta had a long and, to all appearances, happy marriage and they secured the continuity of the family line by producing four children and numerous grandchildren. And it was through his late wife that George had developed an interest in the American Vedanta movement, Betty Leggett and her unmarried sister, Josephine McLeod, had first met Swami Vivekananda, an Indian mystic, in 1895 when he gave a lecture on Vedanta in New York. Both sisters, but especially Josephine, become fascinated by the Hindu religion, their enthusiasm was passed on to Alberta who visited Ramakrishna temples in India several times with her mother and her aunt, travelling there again in 1912 with her husband, George Montagu. Here the couple met the Swami's widow, Sri Sarada Devi, and touched her feet as a mark of respect. Alberta's step-father, Frank Leggett became similarly sympathetic, donating money to various of the Vedanta Society's ventures and creating the estate which would later become the Vivekananda Retreat in Ridgely, north of New York City. Leggett also became the first president of the Vedanta Society of New York.

It was Josephine McLeod in particular who became the most dedicated follower of Swami Vivekananda, she spent forty years of her life tirelessly promoting and funding the spread of the Vedantic ethos throughout Europe and America and giving regular financial contributions to the cause of women's and girls' education in India.

Amiya would have been personally acquainted with Josephine because during her final years, the old woman, much revered by the other devotees, lived at the Hollywood Vedanta Centre in Ivar Avenue, dying there in the autumn of 1949 aged ninety one. Amiya could never have guessed that a few years later she would replace Miss McLeod's niece as Countess of Sandwich.

So it was not by chance that George Montagu visited the Hollywood Centre in 1952, he already had family links to the place and an understanding of its' philosophy. He initially stayed at the Centre for just two days before re-boarding his cruise ship and sailing on to San Francisco. On arrival there, the ship caught fire and the damage causedbytheblazetookfourweekstorepair. WhenhelearnedofMontagu'ssituation, the Swami invited him back to stay at the Centre until the ship was ready to sail. As Amiya put it:

" *Thus it came about that in March 1952 this stranger came through the gates I had entered twenty years before and which I thought had clanged shut behind me forever.*"

During his month-long stay in Los Angeles, Montagu became attracted to Amiya who had been acting as his hostess at the Centre. Although now aged fifty she was still good-looking and animated and to everyone's astonishment the Earl proposed marriage to her. With the Swami's consent to leave the Vedanta, Amiya accepted.

According to John Yale, Prabhavananda was distressed to lose her but felt that marriage to Montagu provided a graceful solution to what he coyly refers to as "Amiya's problem", whatever that was, and that her departure would also be best for the Centre. Amiya herself felt some remorse for having given up the commitment she had made over many years to the Vedanta Society, and was apprehensive at the prospect of being physically separated by thousands of miles from her guru, upon whom she did still rely for spiritual guidance. But Amiya was resilient and adept at justifying her own desires as unselfish and beneficial to others. She told Yale that God had called her to the responsible work of looking after George.

Her fellow devotee of five years standing, Sudhira, recorded, with various catty asides, the momentous event:

"In 1952, we were surprised to hear of the arrival of Lord Sandwich at the Hollywood Temple. When he was travelling in India years before he had been impressed with the Ramakrishna Order, and came to know and revere several of the direct Disciples. I assumed that he had been in Los Angeles for some reason and decided to pay a visit to the Vedanta Temple and a Swami of the Order. What followed eclipsed the scene of Henry having the notion of taking me with him when he left (Sarada had briefly eloped with fellow-devotee Henry Dennison but later returned to Santa Barbara) .

As it happened Lord Sandwich fell in love with Amiya! She, being English, acted as his hostess. Jaws dropped when he asked her to marry him. Even as Americans we could appreciate that according to the levels of English class structure, Amiya, being on the lower end of the middle class, their alliance would be unthinkable. Henry hinted to Lord Sandwich that he would be getting a "lemon" * See Note 7 *but as it is said, "Love is blind." Their engagement with their photographs were in the papers, Lord Sandwich, 76, to be married to Amiya Corbin, 50, and a few other details. As Chris (Isherwood) remarked, in my memory of what he said, the press swarms like flies to light on tasty news and the next day they swarm elsewhere. Amiya's leaving her Brahmachari vows, such as they made any difference in her life, was over- shadowed by the prestige of her up-coming marriage to a Peer of the English aristocracy. Lord Sandwich and Amiya were married. We gathered that the ladies of the aristocracy were appalled. Each one of them had hoped to become the Countess of Sandwich. They never accepted Amiya socially, but she was thick skinned enough to enjoy hosting fêtes and having the Vicar for tea in her status of becoming Countess of Sandwich."*

Sarada's comments smack more than a little of jealousy, maybe she resented her own amorous adventure being "eclipsed" by a woman old enough to be her mother. Certainly her account, with its' sly hints, social snobbery and general bitchiness, suggests that with friends like her and Henry, Amiya was perhaps wise to take her chances with George Montagu. Whether or not she knew or cared about their opinions of her and the marriage, Amiya was soon on her way to England in high style.

It was, as the saying goes, stranger than fiction ~ poor country girl, then Vedanta renunciate, then Countess.

Chapter Four

1952-1962
"Be careful what you wish for....."

The Montagu family motto is "Post tot naufragia portum" which translates from the Latin as ~ "after so many shipwrecks, a haven." It could have been tailor-made for the newest member of the family as she flew back to England with her sister, Joy on a Trans-Canada flight on 9th July 1952. Her fiancé had already sailed home on his return ticket and Amiya and Joy were to stay for a week or so with their sister, Sally and her husband, Bill Hardie at their flat in Holland Park Road, west London. *See Note 1*

On the flight Amiya wrote a short letter to Christopher Isherwood, back in California, in which she confided that the past few weeks had been *"a nightmareish ordeal.."* she went on:

"In half an hour we shall be arriving and I shall begin my part of the sad act in this strange drama. It must be so. Otherwise I could never have torn myself away from swami, my family and all whom I love so dearly. Nobody will ever know the heartache and the leaving wrench. I hope to forget it."
So here I am in this quite small plane which is gradually lowering itself over England.Fortunately I love England dearly, and am quite fond of George, so that between the two some sort of happiness may come out of all this. It is my duty and "it's a cheerio my deario that sees a lady through" So here goes ! Joy says we are over Scotland but I can't see any heather or people playing golf or Scotch! So it must be England, cloudy!"

Even allowing for Amiya's tendency to dramatise, there is genuine feeling in her description of the emotional upheaval she must have experienced on leaving California and the religious movement to which she had devoted what, in the old cliché, are described as the best years of her life. There is no pretence on her part that she is head over heels in love with George and she is fully aware of the odd twists of fate that have led her back to England in such changed circumstances. But, as John Yale observed, Amiya was good at rationalising her own personal desires as "duty" and she was resilient. Her letter to Isherwood, with it's quick switch from introspection to upbeat eagerness to see what the future might hold, reveals a steely optimism which gave Amiya armour-plated protection against whatever life might throw at her. She was not going to dwell on any negative feelings for long.

It had been twenty years since she had last been in England. Her parents were now long-dead, George Sully had died in 1932, Alice in 1939, but Amiya had kept in regular contact by letter with her English sisters. A pity George and Alice Sully would never know of their daughter's unlikely second marriage; perhaps they never even knew of Ella's religious life in America.

Before leaving America, Amiya Corbin and George Montagu had announced their engagement at a press conference in Hollywood, one headline read: "Hollywood Cult Woman weds English Earl," another article on the happy couple appeared in the Los Angeles Times that month, describing Amiya as the British-born secretary of a Hindu religious order. Other newspapers described her as an American citizen, who had been separated from her first husband for twenty five years and was thus, under English law, free to re-marry.

This rather simplified interpretation of English divorce law concealed an unusual side story concerning Amiya's long-abandoned first husband, Jack Corbin.

The UK marriage records show that in 1945 Corbin had married Florence Gibbens, at which time he had still been married to Amiya, which therefore made his second marriage bigamous. The records show that Jack Corbin and Florence Gibbens went on to marry again at the beginning of 1953. The most obvious explanation of their repeat marriage is that Corbin either had not be bothered or had been unable to track down Amiya in 1945 and went just went ahead with the marriage to Florence. In 1952 when he was contacted by Amiya's lawyers with divorce papers, he quickly agreed and then married Florence for a second time in order to make things legal. *See Note 2*

There was a gap of six months between their arrival back in England and the wedding of the Earl and his new Countess. As well as the usual practical arrangements, the divorce between Amiya and Jack Corbin had to be legally sanctioned. By September, Corbin had been contacted and served with divorce papers and on 24th October a decree nisi was granted on the grounds of his adultery, another six weeks had to elapse before the decree absolute was certified.

After a short stay in London with Sally and Bill, Amiya joined George at Hinchinbrooke House, the Montagu's family home in Huntingdon, and they also stayed for some time, before their wedding, at Copse Barn, Wytherston Farm in Powerstock, Dorset. George owned land and property in the area by virtue of the fact that, as Earl, he was lord of the manor of Powerstock. The whole parish had come into the Sandwich family in 1772 when one of George's ancestors had married the Duke of Bolton's daughter. Three years after Amiya's short stay at Powerstock, in 1955, George's son, Victor Montagu, bought Mapperton House near Powerstock, which is now the present seat of the Montague family. In 2006 Mapperton House was judged by Country Life magazine to be the finest manor house in England.

As soon as they arrived back in England, George began introducing his fiancée to his wide circle of friends in the artistic and literary world, one of these was Compton Mackenzie, a prolific and popular writer of the time whose novels were admired by such literary figures as F Scott Fitzgerald, Henry James and George Orwell. Mackenzie is probably best-known for the books Whisky Galore, which was made into a film and Monarch of the Glen which was serialised for television. Following a visit to the author in the August prior to the marriage, Amiya sent Mackenzie a letter begging his forgiveness for having to search for her "truant" cigarette case which had later been found in her car, she thanked him for "the delightful time we spent with you" and for being "so very kind", describing the visit as "one of the highlights of my life".

On 12th December 1952, just four days after Amiya's divorce to Jack Corbin had been made absolute, she and George and were married in Huntingdon Register Office, The witnesses included the Earl's eldest son and heir, Viscount Hinchingbrooke and Amiya's younger sister, Sally Hardie. The couple and their guests returned to nearby Hinchingbrooke House, the Montagu family seat just outside the town, for the wedding reception. Set in 59 acres of ground the House, built on the grounds of an 11th century nunnery dissolved during the Reformation, was a Tudor pile, improved and extended over the centuries. It had been the Montagu home since 1627 (they also owned estates and land in Dorset and Scotland) at which time the family were already influential and powerful. In 1660, a shrewd political move by Edward Montagu further entrenched their position: despite fighting against the Royalists in the English Civil War as a Colonel in Oliver Cromwell's army, after Cromwell's death Edward Montagu helped the restoration of Charles II to the throne - accompanying Charles from the Netherlands when he made his return to England. This switch of loyalty paid off handsomely, Charles II created Edward Baron Montagu of St Neots, Viscount Hinchingbrooke, and the 1st Earl of Sandwich. He was also appointed Admiral of the Narrow Seas (the English Channel). This last honour proved a mixed blessing: in 1672, at the age of forty six, he went down with his burning ship fighting the Dutch at the Battle of Solebay off the Suffolk coast.

The most famous Lord Sandwich was the 4th Earl, John Montagu, (1718 - 1792) reputed to have invented the sandwich by slapping pieces of beef between two pieces of bread because he was too busy, either working or gambling, to stop for dinner. A close friend of Sir Francis Dashwood of Hellfire Club fame and a leading Whig politician of the time, the fourth Earl was a generous sponsor of Captain James Cook, who named the Sandwich Islands in the Pacific Ocean after his patron. On his return to England from Tahiti, Cook brought with him a young native islander named Omai who became a minor celebrity in Georgian England, he was a regular visitor to Hinchingbrooke House where his portrait still hangs.

John Montagu's personal life had one similarity with that of his descendant, George ~ both men took up with women of low social status who were young enough to be their daughters. At the age of forty four, with his wife incarcerated at Windsor Castle due to insanity, the fourth Earl took a fancy to Martha Ray, a thirteen-year-old shop-assistant living in London's Drury Lane; he paid for her education and encouraged her ambition to become an opera singer and when she was aged about sixteen, the two began an affair lasting more than twenty years during which she bore him eight children, four or five of whom survived to adulthood. Their relationship ended in 1779 when Martha was shot dead at the age of thirty-seven outside the theatre in Covent Garden by a jealous would-be lover, Captain James Hackman, who was hanged at Tyburn for her murder. John Montagu was said to be devastated and never recovered from the loss.

Although the matronly Amiya and aged George couldn't compete with such lurid goings-on, another curious coincidence lies in the name of Martha Ray's killer, nearly two hundred years later another Hackman would be a source of trouble for the Montagu family: Ferdinand Hackman was the Montagu family solicitor, executor of George's will and eventually Amiya's co-defendant during the bitter legal battle between her and her step-son over George's will. More of that later.

George Montagu had followed an unremarkable path for a man of his aristocratic birth: educated at Winchester and then Magdalen College, Oxford, after university he had worked as unpaid private secretary to the President of the Board of Agriculture and for six years (1900-06) had been Conservative Member of Parliament for Huntingdon. Following this he had confined his political activities to Huntingdonshire, where for over twenty years he was Lord Lieutenant and a member of the County Council for thirty years,

Apart from his work in public affairs, George's great passion was art collection. Over the centuries the family had built up a large collection of paintings which often contributed to exhibitions of Old Masters. George had also amassed one of the finest collections of French Impressionist and Post-Impressionists works in England, including paintings, pastels and drawings by Modigliani, Cezanne, Renoir and Matisse. By doing so he had become a prominent figure in the art world. He was a member of the Contemporary Art Society and had been a Trustee of the Tate Gallery until 1946.

George also had an interest in writing, including poetry; the year before meeting Amiya, he had published his childhood autobiography in verse entitled "Boyhood" and later dedicated a poem to her in "Gleanings" a book of his own verse published in 1955. * See Note 3. According to his Times obituary, as well as having a deep sense of duty, George possessed a charm of manner and endearing kindness.

Amiya could not have come from a more different background; and it appears that she kept quiet about her humble origins, at least as far as the official records are concerned. On the new marriage certificate her father's name and the fact that he was deceased are both accurately noted, but his "rank or profession" was given as "Farmer", not the farm labourer he actually was. Maybe Amiya did tell George and the rest of his family quite freely that her father, in reality, had been a farm labourer all his working life, a man who never earned more than fourteen shillings a week. He was not even a tenant farmer and probably never owned much more than the clothes he stood up in, a tobacco tin and a few sticks of furniture. Maybe it was the Montagus who then politely suggested that she elevated George Sully's social rank for the marriage records. Maybe. It does seem far more likely that Amiya would have drawn a veil over her poor background and by using the term farmer to describe her late father's profession, could imply he was anything from landed gentry owning large estates to a smallholder renting an acre or two.

No one should blame her if that's what she did. Many people nowadays, public figures included, take pride in their proletarian ancestry; TV shows are devoted to the rich and famous weeping over the poverty-stricken sufferings of predecessors they never knew. But in the 1950s the parading of working class credentials was definitely not the fashion. Social snobbery, although becoming less ingrained, was still commonplace. Years earlier, at the Vedanta in California, when Amiya's fellow-devotee, John Yale, had made the mistaken assumption that George Sully was a farmer, Amiya had immediately corrected him, telling Yale that her father had been "far less than that". But is it likely she would have been so keen to correct a similar assumption, had it been made, by her new aristocratic family ?

Whatever the Montagus knew about Amiya's background, on marrying the ninth Earl the former domestic servant and shop-girl assumed the grand title: The Right Honourable Ella Lilian Amiya Montagu, Countess of Sandwich. She now set about adapting to life as a member of the English aristocracy, a life further complicated by her awkward position of being the same generation as her step-children; Amiya was only four years older than George's eldest son and heir, Viscount Hinchingbrooke.

A less confident woman might have been seriously worried at this daunting prospect but fortunately Amiya, never one to be plagued by self-doubt, rose to the challenge and embraced her new life with enthusiasm. What her step-children felt about the situation is not recorded; they may have welcomed her with open arms, they may have been indifferent or they may have regarded her as an interloper. They could certainly be forgiven for fearing that at best their father's new wife might simply be a harmless embarrassment, at worst she might prove to be a real threat to their own inheritance. The titles would always be safe and the same was true of much of the family's property and income. But the remaining wealth, whether cash or paintings, was within the gift of the old Earl, with all the worrying possibilities that entailed. Amiya's appearance on the scene would have raised eyebrows ~ an unknown American woman, albeit English-born, young enough to be his daughter; what if she turned out to be an opportunistic gold-digger? But balanced against any such misgivings would presumably be consideration for their father's happiness and the hope that his old-age would not be blighted by loneliness. But, in several ways, it must have been a difficult situation for Amiya's step-children.

George also had several grandchildren who were introduced to Amiya shortly after her arrival in England, one of his granddaughters recalls:

"I remember Amiya with great affection. I first saw her when she and Grandpa came down to Bembridge, Isle of Wight for him to introduce us. She came down on to the beach, I don't know what time of year it was. She was wearing a furry coat and high heeled boots, teetering on the stony beach. In a family of quite tough masculine types, who didn't care too much about appearances, she was like something out of a fashion magazine. Curly fair hair and make up and a face smelling of something sweet and exotic. She gave me a little blue beaded bowl, which she said had been made by the Red Indians. I have it on my dressing table now!

I didn't know her well as an adult, I just remember her wonderful appearance on the beach with such clarity."

Though George was still Earl of Sandwich and head of the family, in 1944, he had passed the estate and Hinchingbrooke House itself to his eldest son, Victor Montagu, Viscount Hinchingbrooke, who now occupied the huge old stately home with his wife, Rosemary and their six children, Sarah, Elizabeth, John, Katherine, Henrietta and Robert. George had moved into the nearby Dower House, a large mock-Tudor Edwardian villa and Amiya now joined him there. Built by the eighth Earl and known, rather inappropriately, as 'The Cottage', the house was situated within the grounds of the Hinchingbrooke estate, an idea of its' size can be gained by looking at the 1911 census returns which record ten servants living and working there, as well as the eighth earl and three guests.

The Cottage was a treasure-house of modern art, at the time perhaps the most valuable private collection in England, paintings adorned almost every wall space throughout the house, a small Van Gogh even hung in the bathroom. Many were by Impressionist artists whom George had met years previously in Paris and, according to one visitor, he would talk about the pictures and reminisce about the artists with quiet authority; he still invited painters to stay and one of these was Stanley Spencer who drew a pencil portrait of Amiya in the late 1950s.

Less than a fortnight after the wedding the 1952 Christmas Day party took place at the House, Lord and Lady Hinchingbrooke presided over the festivities to which all the estate's tenants, workers and their families were invited. Presents were given to everyone, adults and children alike, distributed by Lady Katherine, George's seven-year-old granddaughter, dressed as Father Christmas in a crimson dressing gown and hood. An eye-witness described the scene which include her observations of the new Countess, Amiya:

"During Christmas Day we all ate vast quantities of mince pies and drank too much sherry. At four o'clock everyone went to the oak-panelled Inner Hall. This had originally been an open area ringed by the cloisters of the nunnery, but had been covered by a glass roof in the early twentieth century. A huge log fire burned in the grate and the glow lit up the portraits and glittered along the edge of the weapons on the walls. In the middle of the room was the tallest Christmas tree to be found, shining with coloured lights and gay with brightly wrapped parcels and from it came the unforgettable, nostalgic scent of the fir tree. We ate excellent sandwiches, mince pies and Christmas cake . No one, short of being near death, would want to miss such a party and no one did. Grandmammas from the farms sat erect on chairs and watched excited children pulling crackers and scrambling after their contents; smaller ones who didn't like the bangs, circled, enchanted, the glittering tree. One who was obviously enjoying every minute was the Countess. She was American and loved a party. While the Earl, gentle and observant, stayed in the background, she joined in the games with the children, and then, taking pity on the baby, who was polishing the floor with his posterior and becoming more and more of a hazard, she picked him up and gave him a softer perch on her knee. Two days before, the Countess had given a children's' party at the Dower House, which we gathered from our small son's excited and incoherent account, was a party to outshine all parties." * See Note 4

"She... loved a party" that could be a discreet euphemism for all manner of things, but certainly sounds like Amiya, knocking back the sherry, playing with the children; having a good time and not particularly bothered if she might appear a bit undignified.

As Christopher Isherwood had noted years before, although a lively, talkative and generous woman, she could often be exhausting company and, from various accounts, people seemed to find her endearing or irritating in equal measure. It's debatable whether Amiya was simply oblivious to the effect she had on others or whether she did know and just couldn't care less. The impression gained by listened to many hours of Amiya speaking to Joy back in America on the letter tapes, is of a woman with a great deal of insight both into her own and others' behaviour, she doesn't appear to be someone who would lose sleep anguishing as to whether people liked her or not, or as one who would try to adapt herself to please others.

Life for Amiya as Countess included the usual social round of bazaar openings, prizegivings, fêtes and generally mingling with the great and the good of Huntingdonshire. It might have seemed pretty dull after the exotic life at the Hollywood Vedanta, but she maintained close contact by letter with her Guru. In July 1952, before their wedding Swami Prabhavananda had come to stay with her and George at The Cottage and during his visit, Amiya received a letter from E.M. Forster, asking if he could meet the Swami. Forster, author of *A Passage to India, Howards End* and *A Room with a View,* had been put in touch with Amiya by their mutual friend, Christopher Isherwood, who told him of her marriage to George, describing it as being " improbable", he went on ~

" She is, in her own forthright way, a character worthy of the amazing George. Do you know him? You probably do."

It's not clear whether Forster was already acquainted with George but he wrote back to Isherwood from Kings College, Cambridge a couple of weeks later:

".....the Countess Amiya and the Swami have just lunched at my room at Kings with myself and Bob (Robert Buckingham, Forster's gay lover)*Quelle combinaison and quelle chance! All fitted and I feel so happy about it. Earl and another man joined us after lunch and I took them all to the chapel."*

Quelle combinaison, indeed: the pillar of English literature and academia with his married ex-policeman lover, the former kitchen maid turned nun turned aristocrat and the Indian mystic, but they seem to have had a good lunch together. Forster described Prabhavananda as gentle and kind but regretted he had not managed to have much of a one-to-one conversation with the holy man, hardly surprising if Amiya was her usual garrulous self.

Forster had a deep interest in Hinduism, in fact he had been criticised for his attachment to religious mysticism and several of the characters in his novels have a symbolic, mystical link with the past, and a striking ability to connect with people from beyond their own circles, an interesting parallel with Amiya's own character. The two exchanged correspondence over the years in which they discussed philosophical and religious ideas and experiences; Forster would be one of the first to offer his condolences to Amiya following George's death.

Another of George's friends was the writer and poet, Walter de la Mare, who was by now an old man. The couple visited his home in Twickenham and Amiya was a regular correspondent; in 1955, in reply to an obviously lengthy letter she had written to him concerning the celebration of Christmas, de la Mare wrote:

"I was delighted to have your message and read it with intense interest. It seems to me to be a clear, profound and simple declaration concerning so many things that are of significance to mind and heart and spirit."

He also wrote that he hoped they would soon have an opportunity to talk together in person. The writer's last letter to Amiya recalled his singing lessons as a child, and looked forward to seeing her and George soon and "for many years to come". Poignantly, this letter was dated 14th June 1956, just eight days before Walter de la Mare died.

By 1957, George and Amiya were already making plans for her welfare and future home following George's death, a sensible arrangement considering he was he was twenty seven years her senior. They decided that they would take a lease on a flat in London at 7, King Street, St. James's, an exclusive Mayfair address. Writing to E M Forster in August of that year, George wrote:

"We have recently taken a lease on a little flat in King Street, St. James' over Spink's shop which Amiya will have as her home, if and when I pass on. I expect to go up from time to time for a few days without having to stay in hotels. It is quite small and Amiya will be able to run it herself."

In case anyone imagines "Spink's shop" to be some kind of little corner shop selling newspapers and the odd pint of milk, it certainly wasn't. It was the grand Mayfair showroom and offices of one of London's oldest antique dealers. Established well before the Great Fire of London, which destroyed its original premises and occasioned the first of several moves within the city, Spink's specialised in coins and medals and had a Royal Appointment. As for the flat above ~ exactly what "quite small" meant to someone who described a multi-bedroomed, detached house with servants accommodation and stables as "The Cottage" is open to question. The flat is now part of Christie's offices.

Also in question is how much influence Amiya had in this decision - was she the driving force in ensuring that she would not end up a helpless widow marooned at Hinchingbrooke, which we know she found dreary, at the mercy of indifferent or even hostile stepchildren? Was George, aware of the possible friction which might follow his death, the instigator of the London flat purchase - anxious to secure an independent future for his widow well away from his children? It is just as likely to have been a genuinely mutual decision.

Regardless of who was instrumental in leasing the flat, it did provide Amiya with the opportunity to get away from Hinchingbrooke and indulge her taste for London high life. She still had many contacts in California, some of whom, like Christopher Isherwood, were wealthy enough to visit London regularly and she met her old friends in style at the King Street flat and various clubs and hotels in Town. Sometimes George accompanied her to London, as in January 1956, when the couple stayed for two nights at the Cavendish Hotel in Mayfair. Amiya's old friend, Christopher Isherwood, was also a guest there and, with George busy elsewhere, the two spent an evening alone together getting very drunk. According to Isherwood, Amiya regaled him with hair-raising tales of the old Earl's lechery and miserliness, whether her complaints had any foundation or whether they were told more for dramatic effect, Isherwood also sharply noted that she gave the impression of greatly enjoying her new life as Countess.

When Amiya and George were together, Isherwood compared the couple to a comedy double-act, with George as the unwitting patsy; for example, if he said he had been surprised by something or other, Amiya would say, behind his back, that he'd get a bigger surprise when he saw how much she'd just spent on a fur coat.

Isherwood's partner, the American artist Don Bachardy, was often present and also entertained by Amiya's asides which George could not hear, he recalls that these were not spiteful on her part, and that the pair enjoyed a good relationship sharing real affection for each other ~ "a really charming couple", in Bachardy's words.

Bachardy, who knew Amiya well for many years recalls that she "enjoyed herself hugely" as Countess of Sandwich and, although he was unaware at the time of her poor background, remembers her being troubled by several members of George's family who disapproved of her possibly because they were suspicious of her motives in marrying George. He describes her as " a phenomenal character" who was a good friend to him and Chris of whom they were both very fond. He recalls

Amiya as "a non-stop talker, but it was good talk, interesting and witty." "She made us laugh, that was the loveable thing about her, she was always cheerful and funny and always made us laugh." Amiya sat for Don Bachardy several times, in London and California, and he was pleased with the resulting portraits which he thought captured a good likeness of her.

A month later and back at Hinchingbrooke, Amiya and George hosted Isherwood and Bachardy and the writer, Dodie Smith and her husband, Alec Beesley. Smith was the author of *One Hundred and One Dalmatians* and *I Capture the Castle*, she and Alec were back in their native England after spending the war as pacifist exiles in America where they had known Amiya; they were now curious to see the former Hindu nun in her new incarnation and living in what they thought would be a magnificent stately home. Unfortunately this turned out to be The Cottage, described by Smith as the most hideous house she had ever seen, meeting Amiya again proved to be another nasty shock

When they turned up on her doorstep, Amiya was delighted to see Chris and Don who were expected, but froze when she saw Dodie Smith who most certainly had not been invited. After years of having to kowtow to people like the Beesleys at the Vedanta Society, Amiya was not going to waste time being politely two-faced, she enjoyed the social boot being on the other foot and quickly took the opportunity of putting it firmly into a woman she had always disliked.

After effusive greetings and shows of affection for Chris and Don, Amiya coldly looked Dodie up and down and addressed her with the withering comment: "Are you staying for tea – or do you feel you should start back at once ?" Smith was determined to stay to tea, however unwelcome she might be, and later responded in kind by acidly describing Amiya as "a trifle overweight to be dressed in scarlet and wearing deplorable patent-leather peep-toed shoes." Fashion-crime and fat aside, Amiya was monumentally rude to Dodie and Alec. After a couple of cups of cold tea and prompted by George's offer to show the guests his collection of paintings, Amiya unceremoniously shouted to her husband that the Beesleys were going home and swiftly ushered the pair of them out, slamming the front door shut behind them; they barely had a chance to say goodbye to Isherwood and Bachardy, who stayed at The Cottage overnight.

Dodie Smith said afterwards that she found it difficult to reconcile the loud, domineering Countess with the quiet figure who, as a Vedanta nun, had meekly carried trays for them in California.

According to Smith, George, a thin figure in an old tweed suit, was by now very deaf and Amiya talked over him, loudly complaining that The Cottage was a dump and did not bother to conceal how bored she was by her uninvited guests. Smith's recollection may well have been coloured by personal animosity, but it does concur with Isherwood's description of some of the interaction between the couple.

Despite unflinchingly documenting Amiya's faults in his diaries, Isherwood placed great trust in her when he asked her to visit and keep an eye on his widowed mother, Kathleen and his younger brother, Richard who lived together at Wyberslegh Hall an ancient decaying mansion near Stockport in Cheshire which had been owned by the Isherwoods for generations and was part of the estate of Marple Hall, which the family also owned and which was also crumbling through neglect. Isherwood of course lived in California and was not able to visit Kathleen and Richard very often , but his relations with them were sometimes difficult and delegating some of his family duties to Amiya must have been a relief. For all her flaws, when Amiya took on a task, she did it with wholehearted energy; she saw the eccentric pair as something of a project and visited them regularly from 1955, continuing to visit Richard after Kathleen died in 1960 at the age of ninety one.

Amiya put herself out considerably to help the two floundering relatives of her old friend, rushing down to Wyberslegh to help after Kathleen had a serious stroke, even though she herself had only just been discharged from hospital following a kidney operation. Kathleen enjoyed talking to Amiya about her elder son, particularly his religious convictions which Amiya shared and their former life at the Vedanta Society. The old woman was keen on the English aristocracy and appeared responsive to Amiya's well-meant attentions, initially she wrote to her elder son describing Amiya as looking ten years younger than her years and noting her "many acts of kindness"; she was particularly impressed by how the Countess had washed and beautifully rearranged the china at Wyberslegh. Kathleen was probably unaware that this was more a case of old habits dying hard than an aristocratic lady turning her hand to unaccustomed manual toil; as a former domestic servant, Amiya had had plenty of experience in washing dishes, and while some born with silver spoons in their mouths are content to live in Bohemian squalor, Amiya came from a class of the rural poor where cleanliness was a necessary obsession.

After her death Isherwood read his mother's diary in which she referred to Amiya as "that bitch", but he noted that his mother had scarcely a good word to say about anyone, pouring venom on all and sundry. Isherwood's brother, Richard, was an odd and reclusive man, although highly intelligent he had never left home or had a job and was unable to form anything much in the way of relationships, he rarely washed and wandered about in filthy clothes and was given to bouts of heavy drinking and rage against his successful brother. Isherwood wrote several letters to Amiya thanking her supporting his mother and particularly Richard:

"Bless you Amiya darling, may you be richly rewarded for all your kindness... I shall always respect any decisions you may have to make in an emergency. You are so exactly the person who could help him (Richard); and he just loved you and so did mother.... religion of some sort is of course what he needs and you are the person to bring it to him ..."

"God bless you for what you are doing for R. That really fills me with admiration & gratitude."

Richard himself said of Amiya: *"I think her insight into life and the happiness it gives her to see others happy, and her complete lack of "side" are the most wonderful things about her."*

A photograph taken at Wyberslegh in the late 1950s shows Amiya and Richard sitting in the garden; she is relaxed, smiling and smoking a cigarette, he tensely grips the sides of his deckchair with both hands and gazes back at her with a half-demented rigid grin.

Following Kathleen Isherwood's death, Amiya tried her best to encourage Richard into engaging more with the outside world, feeling that up till then he had wasted his life by staying with his mother. Amiya wrote him long letters dispensing advice, radiating energy and presenting a glowing vision of how he and the crumbling house could be reborn if he made the effort. She also counselled the homosexual Richard not to be reckless or indiscreet in his relationships, warning him about the dangers of being blackmailed. She described in a letter to Isherwood how, unknown to Richard but in order to protect him, she had sent a male visitor to Wyberslegh packing because she felt an instinctive dislike towards him and feared he might prove a danger to Richard. She ended one of these letters with the knowing comment that, if Richard liked, he could "tell me to mind my own damn business".

It seems Richard paid little heed to Amiya, they remained friendly but Wyberslegh and Marple Hall, another Isherwood property he had inherited, fell down around his ears and ended up being compulsorily purchased by the local council. Richard died suddenly of a heart attack in 1979 at the age of sixty eight.

Meanwhile, in 1956, George, had suffered a stroke which required admission to hospital. He recovered sufficiently to return home and he sometimes stayed in the London flat where he and Amiya entertained guests. She greatly enjoyed socialising and in February 1958 wrote to Isherwood describing a Valentine's Day fancy-dress ball she attended at the George Hotel in Huntingdon:

"I went as Martha Ray, mistress of the 4th Earl of S. She was shot, finally, by a jealous lover. I'd have gladly been shot quite early in the game by the Humane Society SPCTF (Society for the Prevention of Cruelty to Feet). They killed me as my dress weighed a ton, though quite elegant. She had eight children by the 4th earl, the side panniers of my dress could have fitted two sets of twins!'

There were also hints of her impatience with George:

"Such bondage as we take unto ourselves while all the time we cry out 'For God's sake , give me freedom!

I'm not the best learner in the world of life's lessons, I'm afraid.

Had dinner (in London) on Tuesday with my two bachelor neighbours, (Sir Peter) Churchill could not come. M. Rene Parsin "Le Conseilleur Culturel de l'Embassade de France" & his wife came in last evening for a drink. I'd hoped that their coming would have bucked George up sufficiently to make the effort to come up. Instead, he was hurt because "after all, they are my friends." !

I felt entitled, as his wife, to claim the same relationship & told him so, quite emphatically I'm afraid. I'm afraid G has settled down & will from now on enjoy the exquisite luxury of invalidism – even though the doctor assures him he is perfectly able – physically – to go to London. But there we are. We all of us seek attention to ourselves in one way or another & some there are who will spare no effort towards its attainment. I know one thing for very sure. I have to make my own friends when and how I may. Amiya has to think of Amiya now – no one else will I've found, after six years!"

The letter also gives an insight into the cold relationship between herself and George's surviving son and daughters:

"And damn it when Elizabeth Montagu (George's daughter) once told me frankly "You see, I am an intellectual and you are not." I felt like saying "Well at least I'd have sufficient intelligence not to make such an egoistical remark." She has been the one member of the family who has been in any degree friendly towards me. But I never court her, or any of them."

As Swami Prabhavananda had warned Amiya at the time she decided to marry George:

"Be careful what you wish for..."

So although Amiya spent more of her time caring for George, she continued to visit London, and also made transatlantic flights at regular intervals to visit her old home at the Vedanta Society in Hollywood. During these visits, parties were thrown for Amiya during which she complained loud and long to her American friends about her many tribulations, not least George's increasingly senile behaviour and the sacrifice she had made in marrying him and returning to England . This was all "self-pitying crap" according to Isherwood. At one such party, held in October 1958, thrown in her honour by the President of the Vedanta Society, Amiya began by showing off her collection of new hats and then sounded off at length on the subject of the hallucinogenic drug, mescaline, about which her friend Aldous Huxley had recently written a scholarly article.

According to Isherwood, the usually imperturbable Swami Prabhavananda "very nearly snapped at her". There is a funny side to this last scene: upper class writers and religious devotees who all took themselves very seriously having to listen to the drunken ramblings of a woman they were too well-mannered to tell to shut up ~ not that it would have made a blind bit of difference anyway. Before she left , Amiya asked the Swami if he had any advice for her, he replied simply: "You have made a success of your life." She was apparently as mystified as Isherwood by this cryptic answer and, for once, became silent.

Although he sometimes wearied of her raucous, drunken behaviour, it should be remembered that Isherwood was equally unsparing in his remarks about many other close friends and people he dearly loved. He sometimes wrote his diary entries after drinking heavily himself and says time and again that he wouldn't have written so nastily if he hadn't been drunk.

Earlier in the month he, Don Bachardy and Amiya attended the Hollywood film premier of "Bell, Book and Candle" starring James Stewart and Kim Novak, it had been adapted from a book by John Van Druten, a Vedanta acolyte and old friend of Amiya and Isherwood. Also present was Elsa Lanchester who had a supporting role as a witch in the film; she was the wife of the actor Charles Laughton, who was an old friend of Isherwood's . Lanchester had a track record of disliking other women and a sharp tongue, she once said of the actress Maureen O'Hara "She looks as though butter wouldn't melt in her mouth, or anywhere else." A drink-fuelled Amiya, and Elsa, who was also renowned for hard-drinking, hated each other, there was an inevitable clash between the two women and the evening was not a success.

Interestingly, in a letter to Amiya two years later, Isherwood refers to Laughton as "your old flame", which was almost certainly an ironic joke on his part. Laughton, despite his marriage to Lanchester, was gay but had lived in California on and off for years, including those when Amiya was at the Vedanta Centre. Who knows, Amiya may, years before, have had some kind of platonic relationship with Laughton, which might explain the hostility between herself and Lanchester.

The following month, she was back in London being entertained by Isherwood and Bachardy at Kettners restaurant in Soho, a favourite haunt of Amiya's. They took her out in an attempt to cheer her up after hearing more of the "terrible time" she was having with George. Isherwood observed that Amiya seemed most at ease with "brash and non-U" people like the man who owned the garage where she kept her car, Bachardy added that such was the rapport between Amiya and the garage man that he had half expected the couple to "quite suddenly have sex, on the carpet". It's not surprising that after having to keep up appearances with aristocrats and upper-crust writers, Amiya would sometimes enjoy the less rarefied company of people nearer her own social background. Later in 1961, she would annoy Isherwood by, according to him, turning up drunk and almost wrecking a show of Bachardy's portraits, including one of herself, at the Redfern Gallery in London, although Don Bachardy himself has fond recollections of Amiya.

Back at Hinchingbrooke, George's daughter, Elizabeth, moved into the Dower House to help Amiya look after her father who was becoming increasingly frail. By this time, Hinchingbrooke House itself had been abandoned as a home by the Montagus, they could no longer afford the upkeep of such a large estate and in 1958, when Viscount and Lady Hinchingbrooke divorced, they and their children moved out. The empty House fell into decay which was hastened in 1960 by a disastrous flood started by a faulty fire safety sprinkler system which caused ceilings to collapse and the ruin of antique decorative plasterwork and timber panelling. No one wanted to lease such a ruin, it would have to be sold.

On June 15th, 1962 almost exactly ten years since he had returned with Amiya to England, George Montagu, ninth Earl of Sandwich died suddenly at the age of eighty eight. Just two days before his death he had been sufficiently well and lucid to write to EM Forster about some interesting love letters he had unearthed from the family papers between George's sister, Lady Mary Montagu and Kaiser Wilhelm II. * See Note 5

In a phone call to Swami Prabhavananda just hours after George's death, Amiya recounted that, during his final hours, she had held him in her arms and comforted him by chanting the name of The Holy Mother" (Swami Ramakrishna's widow, Sarada Devi).

The ninth Earl's death marked the end of Hinchinbrooke House as the Montagu family home and by the time his funeral cortège passed out of the gates on its' way to the family vault at the church of St Mary Magdalene in nearby Brampton, plans were being made for the sale of the House and its' estate to the County Council who would use it as the new site for the Huntingdon Grammar School as it remains to this day. The Cottage became the offices of the County Architect and is now an office for the Fire Brigade.

Within a few weeks Amiya had moved out of the Dower House and into the London flat at King Street ~ George had transferred ownership to her some time before his death.

Chapter Five

1962-1986
The merry widow and the bottomless pit * Note 1

By August 1962 the widowed Amiya, now known by the title 'Dowager Countess of Sandwich', was living at her London flat, conveniently situated next to the sales rooms of fine art auctioneers Christie's, at 7 King Street, St James's.

The title of 10th Earl of Sandwich passed to Victor, Viscount Hinchingbrooke, George's eldest son. Now aged fifty four, he had divorced his first wife and married Lady Anne Holland-Martin only a week before his father's death; she became the new Countess of Sandwich. * *See Note 2*

Amiya's step-son, Hinch, as he was known by family and friends, was a well-known Conservative politician; educated at Eton and Trinity College, Cambridge, at the time of the 1926 General Strike his father's influence got him the job of assistant secretary to the Tory Prime Minister, Stanley Baldwin. In 1941 he was elected Conservative member of parliament for South Dorset, a safe seat which he held for the following five general elections. But succeeding to his titles on his father's death meant that he inherited a place in the House of Lords, and so he was prevented, as a Lord, from also sitting in the House of Commons - under the law at the time it was impossible for anyone to renounce a hereditary title and therefore he had no option but to resign as an MP. When the resulting South Dorset by-election was held in October 1962, Hinch openly backed the independent anti-Common Market candidate against the Conservative nominee, a move which did not endear him to the Party leadership, even more so when the resulting split vote resulted in a Labour win.

In 1963, after Tony Benn succeeded in reversing the law, Hinch was able to renounce his title of 10th Earl of Sandwich, becoming plain old Victor Montagu, and unsuccessfully stood as Conservative candidate at Accrington at the general election that year . And although he did not sit in the House of Commons again, he remained president of the Anti-Common Market League and a member of the right-wing Conservative Monday Club. Hinch had already published a book, 'Full Speed Ahead' a series of essays attempting to define the ethics of post-war Toryism, he prefaced his book with a quotation from Edmund Burke:

"Public life is a situation of power and energy. He trespasses against his duty who sleeps upon his watch as well as he that goes over to the enemy."

It's unlikely Amiya read the work, she always claimed to be uninterested in politics, but she was soon to find out to her cost that Hinch was certainly not a man to sleep upon his watch.

Trouble erupted within six months of George's death and the source of it lay in the old Earl's will which had been drawn up in March 1960 and included a codicil added in October 1961. Probate was granted on 7th August 1962 and the executors and trustees then had the responsibility of distributing the late Earl's worldly goods amongst his beneficiaries and arranging the various trusts and investments by which the wealthy ensure their continued family inheritance. The joint executors and trustees were Ferdinand Hackman, the long-standing family solicitor and Henry, Viscount Margesson, the late Earl's nephew.

The will left fifteen paintings to various art galleries and museums in London, Cambridge and Exeter and another nineteen pictures, together with a lengthy list of gifts of money, jewellery, books and trinkets, to friends and relatives other than Amiya.

Then came Clause 5 a) which stated:
"I bequeath to my wife all my consumable stores and provisions and all my motor car or cars and motoring accessories together with the following articles which I also bequeath to her absolutely:

There follows a list of thirty three pictures, three sculptures, one piece of Ting-ware Chinese pottery and a pair of silver plate candlesticks, all identified by artist, subject, type and catalogue reference. ** For complete list of paintings, see Appendix 1

Clause 5 b) confirms that:

"I have already given to her the contents of her flat at Number 7 King Street, St James's, London SW1 which formerly belonged to me."

A codicil to the will added that Amiya would also receive an income for life from the investments and trusts of the Earl's residuary estate. The codicil also confirmed that the Earl had *"made no other testamentary provision for my son* (Hinchingbrooke) *because of the substantial financial provision I have made for him during my lifetime."*

Perhaps Hinch and the rest of his siblings were aware of the contents of the will before their father died or perhaps it came as a horrible shock to them that Amiya received a large chunk of the art collection. Then again, perhaps the shock only came when she began selling the paintings, maybe they had assumed or hoped she would keep them and that they might eventually inherit them back when she died. Whatever the case, there were no moves from Hinch, or anyone else, to challenge George's will for almost four months, it was only when Amiya began selling the paintings that Hinch took issue with it. Once legal proceedings began, they were to last from 27th November 1962 until 3rd March 1966.

Various rumours have floated about over the years concerning the will, the court case and what happened to the paintings.
   John Yale aka Swami Vivekananda, Amiya's old friend from the Vedanta Society, California; writing after Amiya's death, in his book "The Making of a Devotee" claimed that

"... after his (George's) death, there was an extremely messy, well-publicised court case over the inheritance. Since there was, and never had been, any quality of calculation in Amiya's make-up, she defended herself badly and lost."

The first sentence is true, the second is not. Amiya did not defend herself- she had lawyers to defend her; and the case was eventually settled out of court, so legally speaking, no one won or lost. As to whether or not she was calculating, Yale probably knew her better than most.

It has also been said, by Amiya herself according to her nephew, that George's will stipulated that the paintings he left her could not be sold within five years of his death and therefore by attempting to sell them within six months, Amiya broke the terms of the bequest and forfeited her inheritance. This, too, turned out not to be the case.

The first shot in the battle was fired at 11am on Friday 23rd November 1962 when fine art auctioneers, Christie's held a sale of "important paintings by Old Masters". Lot 47 in the auction catalogue, listed as the property of the Dowager Countess of Sandwich, was a picture by the sixteenth century Venetian painter,

Jacopo Tintoretto: *"The Virgin weeping at the foot of the Cross, half length, hands clasped in anguish, in red dress and white veil, with shadowy figures behind."* It was sold that morning for 1,400 guineas or £1,470; Amiya had begun selling the paintings.

In the Daily Mirror four days later, on 27th November, the lead article in Rex North's gossip column "Life in the Mirror" reported that Amiya was selling "twenty two important Impressionist paintings". Either North got his numbers wrong, or he was making a fine distinction between Impressionist and non-Impressionist pictures, or it begs the question: what was she going to do with the remaining ten pictures, the three sculptures, the Ting vase and the silver candlesticks? Rex North's article as a whole can be read as a skilful piece of character assassination: in just a few lines he managed to sneer at Amiya's religious beliefs whilst hinting that they were insincere, implying that the sale was motivated by greed rather than her professed fear of burglars and, by quoting Amiya's own words, hint that she was a gambler and already very wealthy.

It's clear from the article that Amiya had spoken personally to North, which was a dangerous thing to do. Journalists, especially gossip columnists, cannot be expected to behave like trusted friends and anything said to them is quite likely to be repeated in a distorted fashion to suit the particular line a newspaper happens to be peddling. When North approached her, she would have been wiser not to talk to him. But keeping quiet was never in Amiya's nature and talk she did on this occasion, although in future she would be much more guarded in her comments to the press.

If the first Christie's sale and this Mirror article hadn't already sounded the alarms then an advert in The Times on 27th November announcing the sale of Amiya's remaining pictures, due to take place in three days time, ensured they were now ringing loudly. Hinch took swift action. On 29th November, the day before the planned sale, Hinch's lawyers, led by barrister, Nicholas Browne-Wilkinson, beat a path to the doors of the High Court and sought an injunction restraining Amiya from selling any more of the pictures which were valued at around £100,000 *** See note 3. Browne-Wilkinson was later to become a Senior Lord of Appeal, a life peer and Head of the Privy Council. The injunction was granted by Mr Justice Scarman after hearing that Hinch intended to dispute his late father's will. Christie's announced with regret that as the result of the injunction they were obliged to withdraw from the next day's sale twenty six items from the collection of the late Earl of Sandwich; these included works by

Cezanne, Gaugin, Degas, Matisse, Van Gogh and Renoir and a marble sculpture by Barbara Hepworth.

Amiya had quickly learned her lesson about speaking to the press and was reported next day to be "too upset to speak to callers."

Thirteen days later, on 12th December – on what would have been the 10th wedding anniversary of George and Amiya – Hinch issued a High Court writ against her and the two executors of the will, Ferdinand Hackman and Lord Margesson. The writ asked for the deletion of Clause 5a of the will which bequeathed the works of art to Amiya, and accused her of "fraud and undue influence" in the matter of her late husband's will. Undue influence implies that, at the time he wrote his will, George was easily swayed, presumably because of his age, and that Amiya took advantage of a vulnerable old man. Yet there is nothing to suggest that George was senile or did not fully understand what he was doing in 1960 when he wrote the will. It also seems unlikely that Ferdinand Hackman, then the Montagu family solicitor, would have sanctioned a will for a client not of sound mind. Don Bachardy, who met the couple many times, remembers that despite having hearing problems and, understandably not being such a live wire as his wife, George was not senile and that he and Amiya got on well together, there did not appear to be any friction between them. The lucid letter written by George to E M Forster just two days before his death does not indicate an impaired mind.

In the event, Hinch's accusations were never actually subjected to full legal scrutiny.

In June 1964 his action disputing the will was officially set down for hearing in London, but the full case was never heard. Instead, it all turned out to be something of an anti-climax, publicly at least ~ on 30th October 1964 Amiya's lawyers applied to have the injunction restraining the sale of the paintings lifted. Nicholas Browne-Wilkinson, again representing Hinch, announced that "reason and prudence" had prevailed and the warring parties had reached a compromise in an out-of-court settlement under the terms of which certain paintings were to be handed over to Hinch. Browne-Wilkinson also told the court that his client, now plain Mr. Victor Montagu after renouncing his title, had:

"withdrawn completely and unreservedly each and every allegation of fraud and undue influence he had made against his stepmother, the Dowager Countess of Sandwich."

The judge, Mr. Justice Bruce-Cumming agreed to Amiya's application and discharged the injunction against her.

Despite the cessation of open hostilities, the case dragged on for another eighteen months until a final High Court hearing on 2nd March 1966 when the court was informed that Mr Montagu and the Dowager Countess had arrived at "certain financial adjustments." The judge, Mr. Justice Cairns, formally approved the out-of-court settlement between Hinch and Amiya and pronounced in favour of the will in its original form.

Throughout the proceedings Amiya retained the services of George's lawyers, Royds Rawstorne & Co. a long-established London firm; Hinch had instructed Boodle, Hatfield & Co., another London firm and one who specialised in litigation involving high-value art disputes. Without George, Amiya was certainly not in as strong a position as Hinch, either financially or in terms of social connections. And, just as important, she had neither experience of the exclusive and intimidating legal world nor any friends within it. Although self- confident and quick-witted, Amiya was not formally well-educated and would have been entirely reliant on her lawyers and in no position to challenge their expert advice. She had already paid them a great deal of money over nearly four years and would have been keenly aware that going to a full hearing would cost a lot more and with no guarantee of winning. Of course, Hinch was in a similar position regarding his chances of winning but with one huge advantage, he had more money than his step-mother ~ enough to pay lawyers for years in pursuit of what may, in fact, have been a pretty weak case in the hope, if not near-certainty, that he could wear down Amiya in a war of financial attrition. "Reason and prudence" probably owed more to considerations of hard cash than the rights and wrongs of the case.

The terms of the settlement, including details of the "financial adjustments" and the handing over to Hinch of "certain paintings", were not made public. The financial adjustments may have involved a reduction in Amiya's income from the trusts and investments left to her in the will or they may have required her to pay Hinch an agreed amount, perhaps even a proportion of any money she received from any sale of the pictures that she did manage to retain under the settlement.

From Christie's archives, It is possible to get a fairly accurate idea of which paintings Amiya kept after the settlement. Just two weeks after the injunction was lifted, on 13th November 1964, Christie's auctioned Amiya's Barbara Hepworth sculpture, which sold for £1,155. Two more sales followed over the next fortnight at Christie's, on 20th and 27th November, at which a total of twenty four of the thirty three paintings bequeathed to her in George's will were sold; all were listed as "the property of Amiya, Countess of Sandwich from the collection of the 9th Earl of Sandwich". The total amount realised at the three sales was £54,616 which today would be worth almost one million pounds.

These twenty four pictures may not, of course, be the total she retained from the settlement with Hinch. We know for certain, because she told Joy in a tape message, that she sold the Marie Laurencin at Christie's in 1969 for £30 and that this paid for the curtains at her house in Chard. She may also have kept some of them and/ or given some away.

Amiya bitterly remarked at the time: *"Hinch is very much better off and I am very much worse off and that is that."* And while it is true that she ended up with roughly half of what George intended for her, she was still a wealthy woman.

As for Hinch, it had hardly been a resounding victory for him ~ he had failed to overturn the will, only managed to secure for himself less than a third of the disputed pictures, been compelled to publicly withdraw his accusations of fraud and undue influence against Amiya and he had failed to keep his father's art collection intact, which had ostensibly been one of his reasons for challenging the will in the first place.

Amiya made several forthright comments about the case in her many letter tapes to Joy in America, including the following made on the afternoon of Monday 28th February 1966 when she and her sister, Sally had just returned to Amiya's London flat after lunch at the Dolce Vita restaurant; the two sisters are in cheerful mood and report that the crocuses are out and the daffodils in bud but the weather, Sally complains, is "...dull, grey and wet". They begin reminiscing about their mother's habit of stamping on the floor and urging her daughters to "Come on, get up and stir your stumps!" they laugh and stamp their feet in unison then reflect on what a quiet man their father was compared to their mother. At this point, their reminiscing is interrupted by the ringing of the telephone and, following a pause in the recording, Amiya says the following:~

"Well, that call was from Mr. Giles (her solicitor), *he said he would be talking to my counsel, Mr. Tolstoy and he wanted to know, before it goes to court on Wednesday for this business about the will, whether I had anything to say.*

Did I still have an axe to grind or, he said, did I want to say, for example, that I hoped there wouldn't be any ill-feeling between myself and the family & so on. And, I said I hoped the lot of them dropped dead, in fact what I'd like to say about the whole thing is not fit to be repeated in court or for publication because...My God! If I hadn't decided to sell the paintings in the first place,.I'd have had this place swarming with Montagus & I would never have been able to get rid of them, and each one saying Oh, I love this one and I do love that one, oh dear, oh dear. As it is I haven't seen or heard anything from them since George's funeral, nor shall I, I hope. As I told Betty (Elizabeth Montagu, George's daughter) then : I married your father, I didn't marry you and if you want to see me, you know where to find me. But I'm very much better off without them because I do not, and never have done, like leeches and I don't want to start cultivating them now. They have no place in my life because the things that they would have wanted, I no longer have. Hinch is very much better off and I am very much worse off and that is that. Now Sal's gone off to make a cup of tea, but upon my soul _ I am so sick of this whole thing that I wonder I haven't dropped dead myself long ago. But like, Sally says, I should tell Hinch to drop dead instead." Amiya muses that the Daily Express would love to report that she'd blown the Montagus a raspberry in court, but mid-flow she changes subjects and describes the previous evening's socialising when she'd had trouble getting rid of Augustus John's nephew, an aspiring painter who had outstayed his welcome after she'd invited him home to her flat. She says she was rescued by the arrival of Nino. More of Nino later.

In contrast to her bitterness towards George's children, Amiya spoke warmly of his grandchildren and told Joy shortly afterwards:

" I must tell you I had a very nice letter from Johnny (John Montagu, Hinch's son and now the 11th Earl) the other day saying he would be glad when this whole blessed thing is over so he could visit and tell me about his trip to America, which he enjoyed. He said he would be going back to America again on a job of his own, not of his ancestors. He's not a bit like his father, or his grandfather for that matter. I hope it's the starting of a new generation of Montagus. I really sincerely hope so."

And John Montagu himself visited Amiya at her flat at Aynhoe Park where she lived in the 1980s and recalls :

"During the early 1950s we younger children used to walk over from Hinchingbrooke to the 'Cottage' to see Grandpa and Amiya from time to time. I can remember one occasion when we were all there together and there was a photographer taking a family portrait in the garden, and when Grandpa was talking to someone Amiya would say 'Watch the birdie George!' I personally found this a bit irritating, seeing such an elderly person interrupted, but I can now quite see that Amiya was simply trying to achieve a good photograph. And years later I can warmly appreciate the important role that Amiya played and the care that she took with Grandpa over many years, starting from the occasion when his ship's engine caught fire right through until his funeral in 1962."

Despite Amiya's protestations to family and friends, she emerged from the settlement with enough money to live a pretty luxurious lifestyle. For many years she was wealthy enough to afford the flights to California to visit the Vedanta Centre and Joy and her family. Throughout the 1960s, 70s and 80s she moved from the flat at 7 King Street, St. James's to 4 Redlynch Court, Addison Road Kensington and then 24 Monkton Court, Strangways Terrace, Kensington. For a few years from the late 1960s she lived in a large house between Chard and Crewkerne in Somerset. The caretakers from the Kensington flat, Mr & Mrs Gray moved in as her housekeepers. On a tape to Joy, Amiya says:

"You said it was my responsibility to look after the Grays and it is. And it's all been taken care of ~ they will look after me while I'm alive and I will look after them when I'm dead. So what more can you ask."

Amiya's nephew recalled that she eventually bought the Grays a house for their retirement. She tells Joy on Easter Sunday 1969:

"I've not faltered or repented my move to the country, the flat is on the market and I've become a member of a club here in London so I can come up and stay when I like. Oh, and I've bought a new car, a Vauxhall Cresta De Luxe, white with a black interior. So it's the old Sully family motto ~ 'never say die.' The house is on the borders of Chard, in locality of the Whistledown Inn, it's an old manor house with five bedrooms and a large ballroom, altogether far nicer than The Cottage (at Hinchinbrooke) and there's a public park just across a meadow from the house. The asking price is £10,950 and the owner is a Mr Stone who tells me that under the tennis court is an old swimming pool.

Mrs Stone wants to throw a party to introduce me to to local MP & Mayor, which is all a bit much and I have to supply the liquor. We had fun at the Dolce Vita last night, Peter (her nephew, eighteen year-old son of Amiya's younger sister, Violet) is staying and we took Susan, her French friend and the other Peter there to dinner after the theatre. I did my Keys to Heaven routine with Rex & Ricardo; you know Rex, the singer with a beard. Christopher Hogan was there, the film director. We didn't get back here till two."

For several years after George's death, although living in London Amiya also owned an eighteenth century cottage at Blewbury, a picturesque village near Didcot, now in Oxfordshire, then in Berkshire. This cottage, unlike the Spartan places of her childhood, had all mod cons and was about an hour's drive from her Kensington flat.

Amiya loved spending a few days at a time here, away from London; she became particularly friendly with Renee, the landlady of Blewbury's pub, The Red Lion, and spent many happy hours in the bar there, making friends with other pub regulars including local artists, Martin Harvey and a man named Revell.

A frequent visitor to the Blewbury cottage was Amiya's nephew, Peter who for four years, until 1969, lived with his older brother, Tony Morrison a long-distance lorry-driver, and his wife and three sons in the nearby town of Didcot. Peter's mother, Violet died from an overdose of barbiturates at the age of fifty seven; the coroner recorded a verdict of death by misadventure. Her sisters were understandably shocked by Vi's death, Maisie told Joy:

"Poor Vi, it was terrible. We're still puzzled by the whole thing and how it could have happened. Only the week before she'd been to see me in Reading and said she felt on top of the world and hadn't felt so well for years. Amiya's on the phone now talking to Peter, he's only fifteen but already a big chap. It's a real tragedy. But there we are. Now there's only eight of the ten of us left (the eldest sister, Ada had died in 1952 at the age of sixty two)".

Amiya took her responsibilities as an aunt seriously and had always taken a keen interest in her nephew, even before his mother's death, a photo taken in about 1962 when she took him to Madam Tussauds in London, shows the pair laughing happily together. After his mother's death , she made it her business to encourage and support Peter, he became a regular visitor to both Blewbury and the Kensington flat, staying overnight and being entertained by Amiya's friends at various restaurants, theatres and clubs.

At regular intervals, Amiya would drive the few miles from Blewbury to Didcot to see Peter and the rest of the Morrison clan, as improbable as it sounds, the Dowager Countess of Sandwich would arrive in the Bentley to visit her family who lived in a small, crowded house on a council estate in Didcot. Amiya clearly had a deep affection for Peter, in 1966 she told Joy:

"I was at Blewbury at the weekend and on Saturday morning who should come round but my six foot nephew, Peter (then aged sixteen), he'd ridden over on his bicycle from Didcot and it did my heart good to see him. He looked radiant, his cheeks were glowing, his eyes were bright and his teeth were gleaming and he looked happy. Oh and I put my arms around him and I was so glad to see him. I gave him a good talking to three weeks ago and told him that he was a Sully and that the Sullys never say die ~ we accept every challenge and take every opportunity. And he said that since our talk, he felt more settled in his work and happier and he's saving some money, then he gave such a bright smile, he's got lovely, white, even teeth and such a handsome face ~ he's a credit to the Sullys."

In 1969 Amiya reported:

"Peter's coming this afternoon, I wish you could see him - he's working hard, saving money to go to Australia he has ambition and I know he's going to make a success of his life."

And he did. When he was nineteen, Peter went to Australia, married, had two sons and became a successful builder; he describes his aunt as *"the most lovely person you could hope to meet. She was always kind and generous, someone who brought out the best in people."*

In November 1967 the cottage at Blewbury was targeted by burglars who broke in through a back window and made off with Amiya's television set and "some odds and ends", as she told Joy. Typically, Amiya put on a brave face, refusing to be intimidated she continued staying on her own at the cottage. Shortly afterwards she sent a Christmas tape to Joy, saying:

"Blewbury was my citadel and it's been invaded ~ it makes me want to spit! But enough of that, let's get on and sing for you."

Amiya, Sally and Floss then give a rousing chorus of *'Hark the Herald Angels Sing.'*

Amiya had always been interested in antiques, as early as 1960 she had written to Isherwood:

"Since meeting Hyler Whyte earlier this year, I have considered going into the antiques business – as a hobby. HW says I have a natural eye & good discrimination etc. & he encouraged me strongly. And I have been studying up along these lines since. It could be a fascinating hobby."

After George died, for several years she dabbled in the antiques business, buying and selling items which she enjoyed doing, although she never made a significant amount from it.

In 1966, an echo of the past involving George's time as a trustee of the Tate Gallery, marginally involved Amiya when the Sunday Times printed an article in their Atticus column on what was known at the time as The Great Tate Gallery Affair. One of the chief protagonists had been a man named Leroux Smith Leroux, who, in 1963, had been found dead at the age of forty nine.

Leroux was a South African mural painter and art dealer who in 1950 had been appointed Deputy Keeper at the Tate by its' Director, Sir John Rothenstein. A bitter feud soon developed between the two with various artists, collectors and art historians drawn in. Amongst the Trustees supporting Leroux against Rothenstein were the painter, Graham Sutherland and art collector, George Montagu.

In 1954 Leroux was dismissed from the Tate and then briefly worked for Lord Beaverbrook before becoming an art dealer until his death in 1963. In October 1966, the Sunday Times Atticus column quoted from Sir John Rothenstein's newly-published memoirs which included Lord Beaverbrook's accusation that Leroux had swindled him out of £40,000 and that claimed Leroux's death had been suicide. Not surprisingly this caused great upset to Leroux's family, particularly his thirteen year old daughter, Azaria. Amiya had got to know the family through George's position at the Tate and she still knew them well, Mrs. Leroux had phoned her as soon as she read the article and Amiya promised she would write a letter to the Sunday Times, which she promptly did. She read the finished draft to Joy:

Dear Sir, I was present at the inquest of Mr. Leroux in 1963, I heard the verdict, coronary occlusion, given by the coroner. This verdict gives the lie to the statement made by Atticus in the Sunday Times on October 7th that Mr. Leroux committed suicide. This stated as a matter of fact shocked me deeply, following as it did immediately on the accusation made by Lord Beaverbrook. My late husband was a member of the Board of Trustees for the Tate Gallery years and knew, but did not particularly admire Sir John Rothenstein. Mr. Leroux was a close and trusted friend of my husband until his death. Mr. Leroux is dead, but he has left behind him growing children whose intelligent minds are bound to be affected by these cruel statements and may give rise to doubts and questionings which could have quite disastrous effects upon their future lives. Yours etc" Amiya continued to Joy:

"People open their bloody mouths and make statements about things they know nothing about and this Rothenstein, I used to hear George and Leroux talking about him at great length and they had no time for him. At the time I didn't pay too much attention as I wasn't interested. But I told the man at the Daily Mail it was cruel, wicked and wrong to upset a thirteen year old girl about whether her father committed suicide and was a swindler. So hopefully that is what will appear in the Sunday Times next week, I spoke to Hunter Davis, who apparently writes as Atticus and he told me a lot of letters are already coming in and he told the Editor to be on the lookout for my letter and to see it was published."

Amiya's letter was published in the Sunday Times the following week together with a letter from Sir John Rothenstein who re-entered the fray with a letter in his own defence. Leroux's widow made a complaint to the Press Council who made an adjudication which criticised the Sunday Times for *"publication of an inaccurate statement that Mr. Leroux Smith Leroux had committed suicide; that it was improper for Atticus to convert the story at second hand as a bald statement of fact; and that the expression of regret made in a footnote to the letter from Amiya, Countess of Sandwich, was inadequate as a correction and as an apology."*

Amiya spent much time wining and dining her family and numerous friends at West End clubs, restaurants and bars, particular favourites were The Dolce Vita, Flanagan's, The Nightingale, The Gondolier and Churchill's in Bond Street which featured a floor-show with singers and dancers. Churchill's was run by Bruce Brace and Harry Meadows in association with south London gangster Billy Howard. In the swinging sixties, Meadows had the reputation of being King of the West End, one regular during this time said of Meadows: *"Harry, bless him, was... into bon homie and general fun 'n' frolix - and good food and even better booze! Sadly the last of an era. Odd names leap into my mind, Leslie Butterball, Lew Lane (stage manager), Sandra Blair, Jacqueline Jones and the long serving Charles Yates who was a great friend of dear old Bob Monkhouse."*

One of the singers at Churchill's was Glenn Weston, known to his friends as Johnnie, who with his partner Keith, became close friends of Amiya, he recalls many evenings spent there with her. Although Amiya was thirty or so years older than these young men, she had the stamina of a woman half her age and they would all drink until the early hours and then go for breakfast at the Cavendish Hotel. She encouraged the initially shy Glenn to sing professionally, telling him "Do you want to stay a housewife all your life or do you want to be a star?"

Glenn took her advice and he worked on the QE2, toured America and sang the title song on the soundtrack of the 1968 Franco Zeffirelli film, Romeo and Juliet.

Glenn remembers Amiya as "intelligent, practical and full of life". "She was such a good friend to us, a really lovely woman."

"She was such a talker, she could talk about anything and everything, she knew a lot about life. I always loved listening to her."

Another singer booked by Lew Lane at Churchill's during the early 60s was Leslie Hutchinson, known as "Hutch". Born in Grenada in 1900, Hutch was a talented singer and pianist whose heyday had been in the 1930s when he had a scandalous affair with Lady Edwina Mountbatten who reportedly gave him a diamond-studded penis sheath. The affair ended when Lady Mountbatten successfully sued the Daily Mirror for falsely claiming she was having an affair with another black singer, Paul Robeson. Hutch fell out of favour and his career fell into a decline, by the 1960s his glory days were well past although he was reputed to have slept with with Princess Margaret and half the titled women in England. In 1964 Amiya tells Joy:

"Who should phone me this afternoon, but Hutch ~ I don't know if you remember him but he was a famous entertainer before the war. I was introduced to him a few years ago and he phoned to say that he's heard about my accident in Italy and he wanted to know how I was and if we could renew our acquaintance, which no doubt we will do. He was mixed up with a high-society scandal with a very prominent titled lady whose husband is even more well-known, I'm not going to name them on this tape. It doesn't matter anyway. I've suggested we go to Flanagan's next week, which will be a bit of a come-down for him as I believe he entertained them at Buckingham Palace many years ago.

But I'm off for dinner with Tony in a minute, I'm standing here wearing the emerald green dress I wore to the Hilton Tower when you, Floss, Sally and

I went there last week. In fact, we might go there again tonight"

One of her friends from the 1960s remembers that Amiya had an affair with one of the waiters at the Dolce Vita, an Italian much younger than she was, named Nino. Amiya related that for his birthday:

"I took Nino to see Madame Butterfly and then we went up to the Hilton roof garden and that was very nice ~ a tremendous panorama of London, the stars were all shining and I could see all the way where I used to drive back to Huntingdon."

The affair ended in 1965 when Nino returned to Italy. Amiya told Joy:

"Nino's gone back to Italy to get married ~ I wish him well and I'm sorry for his wife." then she laughs, adding: *"I've made up my mind not to miss him."*
But when Amiya leaves the room, Floss confides to Joy via the tape recorder:
"Amiya says she doesn't miss Nino, but I miss Nino on her behalf because I think the days are a bit long and lonely for her."
There might have been others, in 1968 she told her sister:
"It's seven in the morning and I've been up all night talking with someone who turned up at the flat and in a minute he's got to go and take his little girl to school. People do have such complicated lives ~ to say nothing of my own."

But then things may not have been what they appeared because earlier in the year, she had said to Joy:

"Tony and Keith were here last night and they said they couldn't understand why I live the celibate life I do as they said men are still attracted to me. But I do live a completely celibate life, even though last week I had the chance for a good old romp in bed with an American staying in London, but I warded him off by asking about his wife, but it took till quarter past three to get rid of him. I usually fall back on talking about philosophy, that really puts them off! So I could have had a good time, if that's what you think having a good time is, but what the hell, I didn't."

Amiya sometimes suffered from arthritis and she sought treatment from an osteopath, Donald Norfolk, who had many wealthy and famous clients at the time. On his website he includes a profile of Amiya entitled 'From Nun to Night Club Dancer' although he refers to her as a Buddhist rather than a Hindu, it's gives an idea of her lifestyle:

"People have a past as well as a present, and sometimes it can be a shock to discover what they did in their younger days. That thought came to me strongly a few days ago when I was rummaging through a shelf of autographed books which over the years have been given me by their authors. One paper back book – given to me decades ago by a long deceased friend – took me immediately on a trip down memory lane. I knew her first as a patient. She was well known in London, largely because she was regularly featured in the diaries of the gossip columnists. When first we met she must have been in her early sixties, a fun-loving member of the elite Chelsea set whose party piece was to dance on table tops when the evening was in full swing. She was so popular and well-known that whenever she entered a night club or restaurant the pianist or band would greet her arrival by playing her signature tune: 'There is a lady sweet and fair'. (She probably tipped outrageously to secure this privilege.) Knowing her in this context it came as a total surprise when she later gave me a collection of essays on Buddhist philosophy called Vedanta for Modern Man. In the book there were erudite chapters by Aldous Huxley, Christopher Isherwood, Alan Watts and Rabindranath Tagore, and also two pieces she'd written herself when she was a Buddhist nun in the convent at Santa Barbara, California.

She entered this spiritual retreat at a time when she'd become dissatisfied with her material possessions. These had failed to bring her true happiness. Inside she recognised a spiritual void which she longed to fill. If that spiritual desire came from the depths of her own being, she argued, its fulfilment must also come from within. Her ignore-ance, as she called it, ended when she focussed her attention on 'the one God who resides in the heart of all beings.'

Throughout her life she held fast to this belief. But while my copy of the book has a touching inscription, and is signed 'Sister Amiya', I will always remember her as the lively, loving, larger-than-life, character better known to the glitterati and social diarists as the Countess of Sandwich."

Amiya was also a keen theatre-goer and she loved the opera. Her close friend, Tony Newman, who spent much time with her, worked for the Covent Garden Opera House and through him she met several top class singers of the time. Her nephew, Peter recalls attending a party at Amiya's flat where one of the guests was Maria Callas. One afternoon in July 1964 Amiya was in a state of excited anticipation after Tony Newman got tickets for the Covent Garden production of Tosca. Their friend, the Australian soprano, Marie Collier, was to replace Maria Callas in the starring role, after the diva had cancelled her scheduled appearances after a performance in front of the Queen:

"Sally is coming with me tonight to watch Marie Collier who could become the greatest Tosca ever. We're frantic with excitement because we love Marie Collier, she's an adorable person and a great trouper. I saw her in Turandot with Tony. I'm going to send her flowers for tonight from Sal and me, I'd like to see her knee-deep in flowers. I talked to her manager earlier and said to tell her my prayers are with her, she's a wonderful singer and I couldn't feel prouder than if she was my own daughter. Callas callously said she wouldn't sing unless it's for a Royal performance, but I wouldn't like to be in her shoes now and I think she's going to regret pulling this stunt."

The following morning Amiya reported:

"We had the most wonderful evening, I've never seen Sally so excited and happy. Marie Collier was magnificent – it was altogether beautiful. I'll tell you all about it later because it's past eleven and I'm still in my nightdress, haven't got my face on yet and I've got to drive down to Blewbury this afternoon."

Marie Collier was a great success in the performance, one critic praising her as better in the role than Callas.

As well as high-brow musical performers, Amiya kept an eye on the newly-emerging pop scene. Also in 1964, she tells Joy:

"Now last time you were raving on about the Beatles and how they've managed to become so popular, so let me tell you that I have met two of them. Don't ask me which two. The manager at the Dolce Vita phoned and said if I came in through the back, through the kitchens, I would find Beatles, not cockroaches. He said there was a crowd at the front, a load of hysterical girls, but I could get in the back and meet them. So I did. Well they were very nice, nothing obnoxious about them at all. They're a bit scruffy but seem bright enough although quiet, not loud at all. I had a couple of pictures taken with them, one when I'm shaking hands with them and then with me standing in between the two of them. My face is OK but I look big as a house, too fat, so I think I'll cut my body off the photo and just leave my head with them.

Anyway, I think you have nothing to worry about, it's all mass hysteria really, just like Rudolph Valentino except there's now more money about and of course the television is what really gets things going now. But nothing really changes."

During the 1960s, Amiya funded Sphinx films, a film production project. The company produced several travel films of Italy, one of which was for National Geographical. Sally, who took Italian classes to prepare herself for the task, produced the films and her husband, Bill wrote the scripts which were voiced by Simon, an actor friend of Sally's. They all made several trips to Italy, including the exclusive, fashionable resort of Laigueglia, but the films were not commercially successful and the company eventually petered out. Instead of making money, which was the intention, Amiya lost a substantial amount in the failed enterprise, but no doubt much fun was had by all during the making of the films on the sunny Mediterranean coast.

Amiya greatly enjoyed spending money, she loved new clothes, jewellery, hats and shoes, flashy cars and having a good time at the best London could offer. She didn't stint on luxury spending, but she was also very generous with her money, splashing it around indiscriminately, even to those who might have simply been taking advantage. In 1971 she told Joy that Mr. Hughes, her bank manager was trying to tie her hands and purse strings "...because, they say, I've been too generous." Sally and Floss became quite indignant on her behalf towards acquaintances who, they felt, were taking her for a ride. Floss says: *"You really must stop it Amiya. There's plenty of ways people can get money apart from getting it from the Countess of Sandwich. I don't know how people can do it ~ taking your money and then just walking off."* Amiya is characteristically unperturbed and laughs the subject off.

Although she was generous with her money, Amiya resented paying the super-tax imposed by Harold Wilson's first Labour government, this included a 15% surcharge on "unearned income" which included investments and dividends. Her income mainly consisted of what George had left her, which was just the kind of unearned income targeted by the Labour government. Not surprisingly then, in financial matters at least, she appears to have strongly identified with the class into which she married rather than the one into which she was born. She certainly wasn't a champagne socialist. Just before Wilson's re-election in 1966, she complains bitterly to Joy:

"I'm just writing a cheque for £1,446 17 shillings and sixpence to send to the Inland Revenue in Worthing. Mr Hackman sent me a nice little windfall of fifteen hundred pounds out of the accumulation of George's dividends over

the last three years since he died and I have to give it all back except for £3 2 shillings and sixpence. We are an oppressed nation with this terrible taxation and I'm afraid Wilson is going to get back in. I said to Mr. Hackman perhaps I'd better get married again!

(To which Sally cries "Oh, heaven forbid after the last lot!" and they both laugh.)

Amiya kept in regular contact with her old friend Christopher Isherwood and he describes meeting her both in London and California during the 1970s

April 11th 1970 "Yesterday I had lunch with Amiya: she came up to London specially. She remarked that she'd sold a piece of furniture in order to do so but I think she is talking a poor mouth partly in order to convince herself that she must not give money to (her sister) Sally and her other greedy hangers-on. Anyhow I paid for our lunch, which we ate in a gaming club called The Nightingale in Berkeley Square: a peculiarly dreary place, as I suppose they all are, reeking of polite gangsterism: they addressed A as "my lady". A seemed fatter and drunk of course, but with her skin still white and smooth. She rambled on without stopping, about herself; I barely got to talk to her. The funny thing, though, is that she is loveable, her egotism somehow doesn't matter, and though she only talks about herself she actually makes you feel that she cares for you."

December 1972 "Saw Amiya who arrived (in California) a few days ago, much talk of her arthritis and I was surprised to see her looking so well, marvellously fresh-faced for a woman nearly seventy."

February 2nd 1973 "In the evening we (Isherwood and Don Bachardy) visited Amiya, whose present flat is much larger than her others, in a neighbourhood north of Kensington High St. She seemed almost or entirely sober, didn't ramble on, didn't indulge in her usual display of her spiritual and worldly wisdom. Instead, she told us about a man (Keith)who is staying in her flat because he is completely broke and about his handsome boyfriend (Glenn Weston) who sends him money from the States where he is on a singing tour. When we left Don said that he had never realised before what a good woman Amiya is."

6th June 1976 London "We went to see Amiya & her sister Joy. "

Less than a month later, Amiya's guru, Swami Prabhavananda died. She had remained in regular contact with him during the years since leaving California and, despite her frenetic life-style, still meditated daily.

Isherwood's last mention of Amiya in his diaries comes in August 1980 when he was told that she intended writing a letter protesting against a bad review of his book "My Guru and his Disciple" either in The Daily or Sunday Telegraph. He writes: "I fear she'll never write to say so".

By this time Isherwood and Amiya were both in their late seventies.

Amiya left London in 1977 and moved to Aynhoe Park, a former stately home which had been converted into elegantly furnished flats for wealthy retired professionals. Now an elderly woman in her late seventies, Amiya's fast-paced life-style had obviously slowed down a great deal. In 1981 she was visited at Aynhoe by Joy's twenty-year-old American granddaughter, Anne Palmerton who, over thirty years later recalled:

"On my trip to England in 1981, I took the train to meet her and was met by her 'albino' as she called the man with pink skin and white hair. She reclined in a bed during our meeting and was quite critical in our conversation. She was a character! Most clear is the emotional content of the visit, because I felt caught in a double bind of Amiya's making. I was a (perpetually) hungry college student. She invited me to eat a water cress sandwich, cut up in fours. I ate one slice and she invited me to eat another. I ate four slices (a whole sandwich), with what I thought was her warm encouragement.
Afterwards, however, when I returned home to California, my mother showed me a letter from Amiya to Joy, in which Amiya described my eating of the sandwich and called me a pig! Needless to say, that didn't feel fair, and left me with the impression that Amiya had set me up and was making 'fun' at my expense."

What Joy thought of Amiya making fun of her granddaughter is not known; but possibly this kind of ribbing was not taken too seriously by either of the two old sisters.

Amiya lived at Aynhoe Park until 1985 when, at the age of eighty three, she needed help to look after herself and moved to a nursing home at 7 The Circus, Bath. At the home that September she added a codicil to her will, leaving £2,000 her younger sister Doris. Amiya signed with a large X showing that she was now unable to write her own name, suggesting that she may have suffered a stroke.

During her last few years she had became close to her old friend and Vedanta devotee, John Yale, who now lived in France, where he had set up a Vedanta temple. He recalled:

"Her letters to me, and her conversation when we together, were all of home, yes, the old home on Ivar Hill and the new home to be, where her guru waited and to which she was ready and even eager to go."

On the morning of 13th February 1986, at the nursing home in Bath, a few streets away from where she had lived in her teens and not many miles from the village where she had been born, Amiya died suddenly at the age of eighty four. Her old friend John Yale wrote:

"The evening before she had had a long telephone conversation with a friend, during which she had again expressed her readiness to quit this world and "go home". At midnight when the nurse came to give her her medicine, she had had a happy and animated conversation in the same vein. The same thing at five in the morning when she had taken some early morning tea. One hour later, never knowing what had happened, she suffered a sudden, brutal stroke and died instantly."

Amiya left estate worth £22,624, (about £59,000 in today's money) split between members of her family, friends and several Vedanta temples in England, France including her old home for so many years, the Vedanta Centre in Los Angeles.

She stipulated in her will that she wished her body to be used for therapeutic purposes, including corneal grafting or organ transplantation or for the purpose of medical education or research and that afterwards her body should be cremated "without any fuss or family bother."

Her funeral took place at Wycombe Crematorium, Bath on 21st February, her body was cremated and the ashes taken away by friends or family. I haven't been able to find out what happened to Amiya's ashes, not that it really matters; her life itself was the important thing and as the woman herself would probably have said ~ what the hell.

Notes

Introduction: Looking for Amiya

1. Amiya's osteopath during the 1960s recounted the following:

"One day she described a recent encounter she'd had with the motorway police. The report began with the attention grabbing statement: "Yesterday I was going sideways down the motorway." When asked how that could be, she explained that she hadn't been feeling well so had parked her car on the hard shoulder to take a rest. She'd obviously had one or two drinks, for she took the precaution of hiding her car keys, so she couldn't be accused of being in charge of a motor vehicle while in an inebriated state. "I was so lucky", she continued, because soon after a police car drew to a halt in front of her. The men helped her into their van and since the event occurred before the invention of the breathalyser, they tested her condition by getting her to walk in a straight line, and touch her nose with the tip of her index finger. She realised that her co-ordination was poor, so drew an imperious end to the interrogation by drawing herself up to her full height and saying: "Do you realise who I am? I am the Countess of Sandwich." After chatting to her for a while, to give her time to sober up, she was released with a caution."

Chapter Two

"We may be poor, but we can at least be clean."

1. Amiya writing in "What Vedanta means to me" (WVMTM), published in 1955

2. In 1933, Joy married Roy Stewart Graham in Los Angeles, this marriage ended either through separation or the death of Roy Graham. In 1959 she married again, this time to Jack Mitchell, who, like herself, had emigrated from England to California in the 1920s and whose own first marriage had failed. He was the father of the American actor and dancer, James Mitchell. Interestingly, Joy's daughter-in-law, Marta Palmerton, was unaware until 2014 that this second marriage had taken place, she only knew of Joy's first and third marriages.

Chapter Three

"Put can't in your pocket and take out try"

1. 'What Vedanta means to me' by The Countess of Sandwich, 1955

2. Very briefly, Vedanta is one of six orthodox systems of Hindu philosophy, based on the Upanishads, the later part of the ancient scriptures known as the Vedas. It teaches that Man's real nature is divine and that the object of existence is to realise this divine nature through a mystical search , pursued by introspective means such as meditation and spiritual discipline. It also teaches that all religions are essentially in agreement, honours all the great spiritual teachers of other religions, considering them as manifestations of the one Reality.

3. A Long, Long Letter to a Friend by Ruth Ingeborg Folling Tate, 2004

4. Diaries: Volume One by Christopher Isherwood, 1996

5. The Making of a Devotee by Swami Vidyatmananda (John Yale)
   of the Ramakrishna Order of India, 1996

6. According to the Vedic philosophy, in which Yale believed, those who are 'rajasic' in temperament are dynamic and seek to control and dominate others. They value prestige and authority and so seek power, status, fame, wealth and recognition. Rajasic people are never satisfied with their position or possessions – they always seek to accumulate more and enjoy flaunting what they have. In addition, they seek continual gratification of desires (sex, food), stimulation of the senses (music, color, fragrance) and entertainment (parties, functions, festivals).

7. The term "lemon" in American slang means a faulty or defective item.

Chapter Four

"Be careful what you wish for..."

1. Sally Hardie (Amiya's younger sister) ~ born Winifred Edna Jessie Sully in 1906, her name change occurred in early adult life when someone misread the surname of her signature, Sully, as the Christian name, Sally. She preferred the name and stuck to it from then on. On leaving school Sally had gone to work in a fashionable dress shop in Bath - this may well have coincided with the time that Amiya lived and worked in the city at around the time she married Jack Corbin. Here Sally met and married Wilson (Bill) Hardie, an Oxford graduate and one-time Fleet Street reporter, this was another leap in social status for one of the Sully girls; her elder sister Florence recalled that Bill was the first

graduate to enter the Sully family and that from then on Sally had no need to work to supplement the family income. After some years, the Hardies left Bath, with their young daughter Jane, and moved to Kensington, London. On Amiya's return to England she and Sally became close and remained so all their lives. Sally died in 1991.

2. Jack Corbin died in Hampshire in 1956 at the age of sixty four.

3. This poem, "The Fledgling", from the anthology 'Gleanings', privately published in 1955, describes a young bird leaving the nest, soaring heavenward in rapturous song only to be captured and imprisoned in a cage with its' wings clipped. Finally, when full-grown, the caged bird is set free and finds a mate, with whom it builds "a love-lined nest". The analogy with Amiya's life is obvious, George clearly saw her previous life as a Hindu nun as a form of imprisonment, thwarting her chances of happiness, and it was from this that he rescued her.

4. 'Houseful at Hinchingbrooke' by W. Mary Stuart, 1979

5. The letter reads:

The Cottage, Hinchingbrooke, Huntingdon 13.6.62

My dear Morgan,

In going through a lot of old documents and papers here recently, I have discovered a whole collection of letters written by the Kaiser to my sister, Mary Montagu. I think he first met her at Cowes yacht-racing with my father. Why I write is because they may possibly unveil political manoeuvring – the letters come from the period from 1905 – up to the war. I thought you might possibly know of some don at Cambridge, who might be interested. The letters are of course love letters, but they may contain news of historical interest. How are you, I hope keeping well. I have been very poorly the last day or so.

Affectionately, George.

PS We are all very happy about Hinch's (second) wedding. She (Lady Anne Holland-Martin) has a charming personality, Amiya likes her very much & even Rosie (Rosemary Peto, Hinch's first wife), of which I am very glad.

Author's additions in brackets.

Chapter Five

The merry widow and the bottomless pit

1. The History of John Bull a satire by John Arbuthnot published in 1712: "Law is a bottomless pit; it is a cormorant, a harpy, that devours everything. John Bull was flattered by the lawyers that his suit would not last above a year or two at most; John was promised that the next, and the next, would be the final determination; but, alas! that final determination and happy conclusion was like an enchanted island; the nearer John came to it the further it went from him. New trials upon new points still arose, new doubts, new matters to be cleared; in short, lawyers seldom part with so good a cause till they have got the oyster and their clients the shell. John's ready money, book debts, bonds, mortgages, all went into the lawyers' pockets. Here again was a new field for the lawyers,and the cause grew more intricate than ever. In short, nobody got much by the matter but the men of law."

1. Amiya Tapes: August Bank Holiday 1965

Maisie: "We've been out with Sally to look at Amiya's new flat, it's bigger than the last one and with a better view. Amiya and I are two merry widows together, I can tell you. She's threatening to take me to the Dolce Vita tonight to make whoopee!"

2. Hinch's second marriage lasted less than three years, the couple were divorced in 1965.

3. The relative value of £100,000 in 2015, in terms of income or wealth is as follows:

historic standard of living…... £1,861,000.00

economic status…................... £4,672,000.00

economic power...................... £5,517,000.00

Appendix one

Works of art left to Amiya in George Montagu's will

PICTURES

No.	Artist	Subject	Type
1.	Bonnard P	Boats in Harbour, St Tropez	Oil
2.	Bonington R	A Girl seated	water colour
3.	Cezanne P	Study of a Tree	Pencil and wash
4.	Constable J	Study of Trees, Stratford St Mary	Pencil
5.	Courbet G	The Vosges Mountains	Oil
6.	Degas E	"La Sortie de Bain"	Black & Brown chalk
7.	Derain A	Wood at Ollioules	Oil
8.	Etty W	Nude woman reclining, two figures in background	Oil
9.	Gaugin P	A river, tree (left) farm in distance	Oil
10.	Gaugin P	"La Ramaseusse de Bois"	Pastel
11.	Gilman	Still Life	Oil
12.	Innes J D	A Woman seated in foreground, Lake Arenig and mountain background	Oil
13.	John A	Portrait of Miss Lily Ireland, standing; pool & hills in background	Oil
14.	Jongkind J	A sailing ship, leaving Honfleur harbour "Le Grand Voilier"	Oil
15.	Laurencin M	A girl's head in a printed booklet	Miniature water colour
16.	Lepine S	Three boys seated in a field	Oil
17.	Masson A	Beach at Arcachon, figures bathing	Oil

18. Matisse H	Portrait of a girl, "Les yeaux bleus"	Pencil
19. Meninsky B	River Avon, near Fordingbridge	Watercolour
20. Modigliani A	Head of a Girl, hand supporting chin "Marthe"	Oil
21. Modigliani A	Self-portrait inscribed "Poverino to prigione"	Pencil
22. Monticelli A	Group of four figures, woodland background "Les Baigneuses"	Oil
23. Nash P	A woodland landscape "March Woods"	Water colour
24. Renoir A	Coast scene, south France	Oil
25. Renoir A	Portrait of Claude Renoir (son of the artist)	Oil
26. Renoir A	Portrait of a woman (left) and a child(right)	Oil
27. Segonzac de A D	View of St Tropez, trees, gulf and mountains in distance	Oil
28. Smith, Sir M	Still life; group of dahlias, crimson background	Oil
29. Smith Sir M	Portrait of a Girl, half-length (left), crimson background	Oil
30. Steer P W	The River Severn at Bridgnorth	Oil
31. Tintoretto Il	The Virgin at the Cross, half-length (left), hands clasped	Oil
32. Van Gogh V	An Orchard, trees in foreground	Charcoal
33. Wood C	Still life, daisies in a lustre jug	Tinted Oil

SCULPTURE

34. Halbout G	A nude boy crouching	Bronze
35. Hepworth B	A torso, three quarters length	Irish bog marble
36. Kogan M	A nude woman kneeling	Plaster

POTTERY

37. Chinese School	A vase, oval, base narrow, V-shaped neck 13" high	Ting-ware

Appendix two

Children of George and Alice Sully

George Sully 1864 -1932 m   Alice Mary Routley 1870 - 1939

1. Ada Blanche	1890 - 1952
2. Elsie Maria	1892 - 1893
3. Eva May (Maisie)	1894 - 1978
4. Ivy Maud (Joy)	1896 - 1986
5. Hilda Fanny	1898 - 1976
6. Florence Amy (Floss)	1900 - 1985
7. Ella Lilian (Amiya)	1902 - 1986
8. Doris Alice Emma	1904 - 1993
9. Winifred Edna Jessie (Sally)	1906 - 1991
10. Violet Irene Gwendoline	1908 - 1965
11. Kathleen Phyllis Annie	1910 - 1996

In addition to the girls listed above, the couple had four boys who were all either stillborn or died soon after birth.

Appendix three

Children of George Montagu and Alberta Sturges

George Charles Montagu 1873 -1962 m Alberta Sturges 1877 - 1951

1. Alexander Victor Edward Paulet Montagu (Viscount Hinchingbrooke)	1908 - 1995
2. William Drogo Sturges Montagu	1908 -1940
3. Mary Faith Montagu	1911 - 1983
4. Elizabeth Montagu	1917 – 2006

Acknowledgements

I am grateful to many people for their generous help, in various ways, with this book:

Sister Anandaprana, Don Bachardy, Christie's archives, Peter Chart, Zoë Draper for the design of this book, Martin Emerson for all his photographic work, Robert Emerson, Kate Hunloake, Barbara Jackson, John Montagu, Donald Norfolk, Ivan Palmer, Anne Palmerton, Dr. Kajal Patel, Pam Richardson, Jane and Michael Shuttlewood, Mary Toase, Dr. David Turner, Nancy and Bill Warner, Glenn (Johnnie) Weston, Mary Whitsitt.

Apologies if I have forgotten anyone and any errors are my own.

Also the following individuals and institutions for allowing use of their materials:

Mary Toase for use of extracts from "Flaxen Hair and Red Pinafores ~ Random Memories of a Country Childhood";

Huntington Library, Santa Monica, California, USA for use of extracts from Amiya's letters to Christopher Isherwood;

Kings College, Cambridge for use of extracts from George Montagu's letters to EM Forster;

Harry Ransom Research Center, University of Texas at Austin, for use of extracts from letters to Amiya from Walter de La Mare, Aldous Huxley and E M Forster;

The Vedanta Society of Southern California for the use of photographs, with particular thanks to Darshann.

Last but not least, to my dear old friend, the late Reg Weston, journalist, for his enthusiasm and interest in this project and his old watchword "publish and be damned". I'm sorry he never got to read this book and even sorrier I wasn't able to rely on his advice and editing skills, this book is the poorer for it.

Amiya shortly after her arrival in California, 1930

Amiya's parents, George Sully and Alice Routley, shortly after their wedding in 1889.

George and Alice Sully with three of their younger daughters in 1915, all dressed in their Sunday best. Note the rag mat under their feet. Winifred, aged ten, seated between her parents; Kathleen, aged five, to her father's right and Doris, aged twelve, on his left. All the older girls, including Amiya, were by this time working away from home.

In the garden at the Vedanta Centre of Southern California, Ivar Avenue, Hollywood Amiya's home for twenty years: she is standing on the right behind the seated Swami Prabhavananda and Sister Lalita, 1936

The guru with his entourage; Swami Prabhavananda with Amiya to his right, Joy (Amiya's elder sister) in the foreground with Sister Prabhaprana to her left, 1948.

1940. In the Ivar Avenue Centre: left to right, Sister Lalita, Swami Prabhavananda and Amiya.

The devotees outside the Ivar Avenue temple in June 1952. Amiya is seated in the centre of the front row between Sisters Prabha on her right and Sarada on her left. Christopher Isherwood is standing 4th from the left in the back row with John Yale on his left.

"Hollywood Cult Woman weds English Earl! "Amiya and George Montagu, 9th Earl of Sandwich pictured following their engagement in 1953.

Hinchingbrooke House, Huntingdon. Family seat of the Earls of Sandwich until 1963.

Drawing of Amiya by Stanley Spencer.

Amiya at Hinchingbrooke House, February 1958, garbed in 18th century fancy dress as Martha Ray, the ill-fated mistress of the 4th Earl of Sandwich, shot dead by a jealous admirer. Note the pictures from George's collection displayed on the walls, which were later to cause so much trouble.

Amiya and George after five years of marriage, 1957.

Amiya performing her duties as Countess of Sandwich ~ presenting a prize at the County Show, Huntingdon, 1961.

The Dowager Countess with three of her sisters in 1962. Left to right: Vi, Joy, Floss and Amiya.

The nine surviving Sully sisters, 1962. Front row, left to right: Floss, Doris, Maisie, Sally; back row: Hilda, Joy, Amiya, Vi and Kath. Ada, the eldest sister , had died ten years previously.

Amiya at the Beverly Hills Hotel with Sir Alec Guinness, 1958.

Living it up at Churchill's nightclub, New Bond Street, London, 1965: Amiya with her arm around her close friend, singer, Johnnie (Glen Weston). The owner of Churchill's, Lew Lane, is seated at the far right of the photo.

Amiya with friends, Johnnie and Keith at the Dolce Vita, early 1970s. Still drinking champagne and dancing on the tables until well into her sixties.

Amiya aged 78 on her last visit to the Ivar Avenue vedanta, Los Angeles, 1980.